Faculty Mentoring

The Power of Students in Developing Technology Expertise

A volume in
Research Methods for Educational Technology
Series Editors: Walt Heinecke and Elizabeth Langran

Research Methods for Educational Technology

Walt Heinecke and Elizabeth Langran
Series Editors

Methods of Evaluating Educational Technology
Edited by Walt Heinecke and Laura Blasi

Qualitative Research Methods for Education and Instructional Tech.
By Mukta Jost and Rema Nilakanta

What Should Teachers Know about Technology: Perspectives and Practices
Edited by Yong Zhao, Michigan State University

Technology and Assessment: The Tale of Two Interpretations
By Michael Russell, Boston College

Faculty Mentoring: The Power of Students in Developing Technology Expertise
Edited by Ann D. Thompson, Hsueh-Hua Chuang, and Ismail Sahin

Faculty Mentoring

The Power of Students in Developing Technology Expertise

Edited by

Ann D. Thompson
Hsueh-Hua Chuang
Ismail Sahin

IAP
INFORMATION AGE PUBLISHING

Charlotte, NC 28271 • www.infoagepub.com

Library of Congress Cataloging-in-Publication Data

Faculty mentoring : the power of students in developing technology expertise / edited by Ann D. Thompson, Hsueh-Hua Chuang, Ismail Sahin.
p. cm. – (Research methods for educational technology)
Includes bibliographical references.
ISBN-13: 978-1-59311-570-8 (pbk.)
ISBN-13: 978-1-59311-571-5 (hardcover) 1. Mentoring in education. 2. College teachers–In-service training. 3. Teacher-student relationships. 4. Educational technology–Study and teaching. 5. Information technology–Study and teaching. 6. Technological literacy–Study and teaching. I. Thompson, Ann (Ann D.) II. Chuang, Hsueh-Hua. III. Sahin, Ismail.
LB1731.4.F33 2006
378.1'73–dc22

2006029518

Printed and bound by CPI Group (UK) Ltd, Croydon, CR0 4YY

CONTENTS

SERIES EDITORS' PREFACE

Technology is on its way to becoming ubiquitous in education. In addition, more and more evidence is suggesting that technology, when properly infused into teaching and learning, has a significant and positive effect on student learning. In a national study examining the relationship between pedagogical approach and technology use based on NAEP test scores as the outcome variable, Wenglinsky (2005) found that students perform better in classrooms taught by teachers employing technology with constructivist teaching methods. Didactic teachers are prone to use technology for drill and practice, while constructivist teachers are more likely to use technology for real-world, problem solving. He concludes: "When technology is used in concert with constructivist teaching practices, students tend to perform well; and when it is used in concert with didactic practices, they do not." (p. 78).

However, one of the most significant stumbling blocks to the integration of technology into American public schools has been a lack of training for teachers. Many teachers do not feel confident or prepared to integrate technology into their content teaching. Currently we are in a period of significant turnover in the population of our nation's teachers (NCES, 1998). Teacher education programs in colleges of education will continue to serve as the nexus for teacher preparation, change and innovation in education. New teachers trained in teacher education programs will be faced with significant challenges to innovate with technology. What are we doing to prepare teachers to effectively integrate technology into instruction?

The Preparing Tomorrow's Teachers for Technology (PT3) program was the largest federal program ever to address this problem. Since 1999 it has funded innovative approaches to train preservice teachers to use technology in instruction. There were several strands of technology innovation pursued by grantees such as course redesign, E-portfolios, state-wide systemic approaches, provision of technology tools including video learning,

Faculty Mentoring: The Power of Students in Developing Technology Expertise, pages vii–ix

and faculty development. Faculty development approaches developed through PT3 initiatives included: mentoring, workshops, design teams, and one-on-one tutoring approaches (PT3.org, 2006). I am happy to introduce two contributions to this Series, *Community of Designers* edited by Punya Mishra and *Faculty Mentoring: The Power of Students in Developing Technology Expertise*, edited by Ann Thompson, Hsueh-Hua Chuang, and Ismail Sahin. The approaches you will read about in these books are excellent examples of the way in which colleges of education are implementing design teams and mentoring initiatives in order to promote the integration of technology in teacher education.

While there were many approaches to technology integration funded in the PT3 program, the mentoring of teacher education faculty received significant attention in many projects. The theory upon which these innovative approaches were based is a sound one. If teacher education faculty could be prepared to integrate technology into their courses, preservice teachers would be seamlessly exposed to technology integration; there would be a multiplier effect as faculty influenced the practice of thousands of teachers every year. The challenge is to find an approach to effectively encourage faculty to integrate technology into their instruction of preservice teachers. This requires significant thought and a theoretically reasoned approach to the task.

In *Faculty Mentoring; The Power of Students in Developing Technology Expertise*, Ann Thompson and her colleagues at Iowa State University's College of Human Sciences detail the technology mentoring program focused on individualized one-to-one technology assistance for faculty. Their approach focused the creation of communities of support with technology-savvy students providing one-on-one assistance for faculty. Their approach was theory-based, drawing on Rodgers Diffusion of Innovations, Bandura's (1977) Social Learning Theory, and Hall and Hord's (1987) Concerns-Based Adoption Model (CBAM). The book portrays seven case studies of one-on-one faculty mentoring and presents lessons about this approach to faculty technology integration and change. The cases provide linkages to the K–12 context as well. This book also offers excellent insight for other programs seeking to implement faculty mentoring programs.

The authors remind us of an important lesson: Innovation in education, whether technology-based or not, is about people. Individual innovation occurs in a social context as a sociological phenomenon. In technology innovation in higher education, community matters. Mentoring pairs thrive in a community of mentoring pairs. Administrative vision, leadership and entrepreneurship are also key ingredients for the success of mentoring programs.

Sadly, the PT3 program has been discontinued and the funding for technology integration and preparation has been continually cut in the

Enhancing Education Through Technology (EETT) provision of the No Child Left Behind (NCLB) Act. The support for technology in education reflected in the EETT provisions of Title II, Part D of NCLB is itself at risk as we write this introduction. It is particularly sad when, as presented in this volume, efforts to develop innovative ways of changing faculty practice and therefore provide modeling of effective technology integration for thousands of teachers have been so successful, thanks in part to federal funding through such programs as PT3. Children will be left behind if policy makers fail to make the commitment to technology training for educators at all levels of the system. As Thompson and her colleagues illustrate in this volume, teacher educators are doing their part to turn federal funding into successful practice.

—Walt Heinecke
Elizabeth Langran,
Series Editors
Center for Technology and Teacher Education
Charlottesville, VA
June, 2006

REFERENCES

Bandura, A. (1977). *Social learning theory*. Englewood Cliffs, NJ: Prentice Hall.

Hall, G.E., & Hord, S.M. (1987). *Change in schools: Facilitating the process*. New York, NY: State University of New York Press.

National Center for Education Statistics, (1998). The Baby Boom Echo Report. Retrieved from http://www.qualityteachers.org/shortage/stats.htm, June 7, 2006.

Wenglinsky, H. (2005). *Using technology wisely: The keys to success in schools*. New York: Teachers College Press.

PREFACE

Ann Thompson

The purpose of this book is to describe the approach and process involved in a program designed to assist faculty in acquiring technology skills and to apply these skills in constructing meaningful learning-centered applications. Most educators will agree that the challenge of developing faculty technology expertise is a major and crucial one for colleges and universities. As early as 1988 it became apparent that teachers were not prepared to use new technologies coming into their classrooms (OTA, 1988). Since then, despite the reduction in the student to computer ratio by more than half (NCES, 2000; Rowand, 2000), teachers still report being largely unprepared to use them with students (NCES, 1999; NSBF, 2002). Many stakeholders in education have pointed to teacher education programs for failing to prepare their pre-service teachers to use new technologies in their classrooms (NCES, 1999). Many studies began to explain the failure of teacher education programs to adequately prepare pre-service teachers to use technology by the inability of faculty in these programs to model effective uses of technology in their own courses (Carlson & Gooden, 1999; OTA, 1995). It became apparent that if teacher education programs were going to be effective in preparing pre-service teachers to use technology with students in K–12 schools, they were going to have to prepare the faculty in universities and colleges to use technology with their own students first.

Faculty in the Department of Curriculum and Instruction at Iowa State University began to address the need for faculty to be prepared to use technology in the late 1980s and early 1990s. Early work with faculty and technology typically included workshops on particular technology topics. In general, these workshops tended to focus on learning technology, not using the technology to improve teaching and learning. It was also difficult

Faculty Mentoring: The Power of Students in Developing Technology Expertise, pages xi–xiv to get faculty members to participate in the workshops, and many faculty members who agreed to participate did not complete the staff development because the programs did not meet their needs. The approach to faculty development described in this book grew out of the realization that higher education faculty members needed an approach that was centered on their individual needs and that change theory (Rogers, 2003) provided a strong base for designing such a program. At Iowa State University, that approach would become known as the faculty technology-mentoring program and would be one of the first of its kind in the country.

The approach we present in this book focuses on the need for individualized one-on-one technology assistance for faculty, combined with the need for creating communities for sharing and support. This book contains a series of stories about technology-savvy students working with faculty. Based on Roger's Diffusion of Innovations Theory and also using elements of Social Learning Theory (Bandura, 1977) and the Concerns-Based Adoption Model (Hall & Hord, 1987), the technology mentoring program emphasizes meeting faculty where they are in terms of technology use and establishing social learning networks among faculty and student mentors. Each story is unique and each provides different insights into the complex implementation of faculty development projects.

This book is intended for educators who are working to lead the meaningful integration of technology into higher education and K–12 environments. The detailed stories provide useful knowledge and background for K–12 educators, higher education educators, and trainers in business and industry who are faced with the challenge of helping people learn to use technology effectively.

Our technology mentoring program began in 1991 and arose out of the need to provide more effective technology training experiences for the faculty in a large teacher education department. The original program developed from very practical considerations. It had become apparent that our workshop approach was not working and that faculty needed more individual attention. Given limited resources, the idea of using graduate students to provide the one-on-one experiences was especially appealing.

Thus, the program began with the offering of the first graduate course, Technology in Teacher Education (CI610). As described in detail in Chapter 1, the seminar course included readings and discussions on issues in technology in teacher education as well as a field component. For the field component, students were asked to mentor a teacher education faculty member for one hour each week during the semester. In the seminar class, the discussions were centered on both current readings and the mentoring experiences of each of the students.

The first semester of our mentoring experiment was successful, both from the perspectives of the mentors and the mentees. Faculty participants were generous in their praise of the model, and the graduate students made it clear that mentoring was an extremely valuable experience for them. Although we have changed and adapted our model over the years, the basic structure remains much the same. In fourteen years, we have had more than 100 graduate students work as mentors and more than 50 faculty members participate as mentees. Many of our graduate students have gone on to establish similar programs at colleges and universities around the world.

The success of the program and the enthusiasm of the participants provided the motivation for the creation of this book. Although the mentoring idea is a very simple one, actual practice is far more complex. We hope that having the opportunity to share the experiences of several of our mentoring pairs will help others understand and apply the idea. In *Faculty Mentoring: The Power of Students in Developing Technology Expertise*, seven mentoring stories are shared. Each provides a different perspective on the complex interactions involved in the change process, and each should provide valuable insight for readers who are interested in this type of program.

Chapters 1, 2 and 3 provide the context, theoretical base and related literature for the mentoring stories. The context for the mentoring program is detailed in Chapter 1; the theoretical base for the program is described in Chapter 2 and the current work on technology mentoring is reviewed in Chapter 3. Chapters 4 to 10 each present the unique story of a mentoring experience. The first story (Chapter 4) describes an experience of mentoring a senior professor who had not previously used computer technology in his teaching and includes his perspective on the experience. This story offers a useful perspective on work with faculty who have had limited experience with technology. In Chapter 5, the story told emphasizes the value of the program in creating a sense of belonging from the international graduate student's perspective. Although the value of the program for the graduate student mentors is a theme in each of our stories, this topic is especially strong in Chapter 5. Chapter 6 features the collaborative efforts of the student mentor and a faculty mentee using a distance education system, WebCT, to design an online course and emphasizes the implementation stage of the adoption process. Chapter 7 focuses on addressing a faculty mentee's concerns in the technology integration process. Chapters 8-9 each relate stories of generalizing the university mentoring experience to the K–12 environment. In each of these two chapters, one of the mentees is a K–12 classroom teacher. These chapters describe how the basic mentoring approach developed with higher education faculty is expanded and adjusted for the K–12 environments and each of the chapters addresses the influence of one-on-one mentoring on the diffusion process in the K–12 environment. Chapter 10 presents another faculty mentoring case with a senior faculty member, emphasizes the use of literature on the mentoring process and provides literature-based suggestions for the further development of faculty mentoring programs.

Chapter 11 includes a discussion of the major common themes found in the cases presented in the book and thus provides specific direction for others working with mentoring programs. Finally, we return to the stories of the authors through presenting a short epilogue for each of the authors and stories. One of the powerful aspects of these stories is that each of the authors continued his/her mentoring work after the mentoring semester was complete. Some went on to begin a similar program in a different setting, some continued their relationships with their mentees, some were offered job opportunities because of their mentoring experience, and some are continuing to work with our mentoring project as leaders. The epilogue provides a brief description of each of the authors of this book and strong evidence of the value of a mentoring program for the students involved in the program.

We hope that readers will enjoy and learn from our stories. The stories weave together to describe the growth of communities of learners centered on determining effective uses of technology in teacher education. The emerging communities of learners are non-hierarchical in nature and provide both expected and unexpected benefits for students and professors alike.

REFERENCES

Bandura, A. (1977). *Social learning theory*. Englewood Cliffs, NJ: Prentice Hall.

Carlson, R., & Gooden, J. (1999). Are teacher preparation programs modeling technology use of preservice teachers? *ERS Spectrum, 17*(3), 11–15.

Hall, G.E., & Hord, S.M. (1987). *Change in schools: Facilitating the process.* New York, NY: State University of New York Press.

National School Boards Foundation (NSBF, 2002). *Are We There Yet? Research and Guidelines on School's Use of the Internet.* Retrieved April, 23,2004 from http:www.nsfb.org/thereyet/fulltext.htm

Office of Technology Assessment (OTA). (1988). *Power on! New tools for teaching and learning.* Washington, DC: United States Government Printing Office. (ERIC Document Reproduction Service No. ED 295677).

Office of Technology Assessment (OTA). (1995). Teachers and technology: Making the connection. (Report no. OTA-HER-616). Washington DC: Government Printing Office.

Rogers, E.M. (2003). *Diffusion of innovations* (5th ed.). New York, NY: Free Press.

Rowand, C. (2000). *Teacher use of computers and the Internet in public schools* (NCES 2000-090). Washington, DC: U.S. Department of Education, National Center for Education Statistics.

U.S. Department of Education, National Center for Educational Statistics (NCES, 1999). *Teacher quality: A report on the preparation and qualifications of public school teachers.* Washington, DC: NCES 1999-080.

U.S Department of Education, National Center for Educational Statistics (2000). *Internet in U.S public schools and classrooms: 1994–1999.* Washington, DC: NCES 2000-086.

CHAPTER 1

HISTORY OF THE FACULTY TECHNOLOGY MENTORING PROGRAM

Ann Thompson

As schools and colleges of education work to meaningfully integrate technology into their curricula, the major challenge is clearly the need to educate faculty in the area of technology use. Even the challenge of acquiring equipment appears smaller than the challenge of working with faculty. In the early 1990s, members of the Department of Curriculum and Instruction at Iowa State University began to develop approaches to working with faculty to assist in their use of technology throughout the teacher education program. The stories related in this book all come from work in the early years of the 21st century; yet they are grounded in the early history of the department's efforts to integrate technology throughout the program. In this chapter, I will tell the story of the early years in order to set the context for the cases described in later chapters. The context described is an essential piece in understanding the mentoring program. Part of this context is the fact that the stories related in this book come out of a mentoring program that has been in existence for fourteen years. The long history and the lessons learned from this program will be useful to other programs in the early and middle stages of developing faculty mentoring programs.

One of the underlying assumptions of the mentoring cases described in this book is that young people bring an exciting expertise to the world of

Faculty Mentoring: The Power of Students in Developing Technology Expertise, pages 1–12

technology and that, as educators, we must recognize and celebrate this expertise. Several educators have suggested that young people are natives in the world of technology, whereas older generations are immigrants to this world of technology (November, 2001). I believe that this is an interesting idea worth exploring and developing. As immigrants to the world of technology, members of the older generations know what it is to learn without the benefit of technology. Many of us wrote long papers, thesises, and dissertations on typewriters. For us, technology is a relatively new world. For younger generations, technology is a natural tool that has always been there. Much of what we describe in this book is the story of natives helping the immigrants discover and understand powerful uses of technology. Although the mentoring relationships described here move away from traditional views of mentors as older people advising younger people, the pairings described all involve people more experienced with technology advising people with less experience. As the reader will see, these relationships tend to turn into powerful learning experiences for both mentor and mentee.

A second underlying assumption for our work is the importance of both change and social learning theory in guiding our work. As described by Sahin in Chapter 2, the primary guiding theory for our work is Rogers' Diffusion of Innovations theory (2003). Rogers' theory emphasizes the importance of understanding stages in the decision process of adopting an innovation and of showing the five important attributes of the innovation. Our individualized faculty development program is designed to pay special attention to assisting faculty in their progression through Rogers' innovation-decision stages. It also provides faculty with the attributes of innovations of instructional technologies to help them adopt these technologies quickly and effectively. In addition, Rogers emphasizes the importance of communication and social systems in the diffusion of an innovation and this emphasis has guided the focus upon personal relationships and formation of learning communities in our work.

THE DEPARTMENT

The Department of Curriculum and Instruction (C&I) is the center of teacher education at Iowa State University. The department is the academic home of 1000 undergraduate majors in elementary education and about 400 students who are earning credentials in secondary education. The secondary education students all have content area majors, such as history or English, in other departments. They take some of their education courses in the Department of Curriculum and Instruction and some in their content area department. In addition to the undergraduate programs, the department also has a large graduate program with approximately 200 students earning advanced degrees. About 80% of the graduate students in the department earn degrees that emphasize applications of educational technology.

The C&I faculty include approximately 35 full time, tenure-track faculty and about 15 temporary faculty. In addition, approximately 15 more faculty members have joint appointments in the department, with the larger percentage of their appointment in their content area department.

Since the 1970s, the department of C&I has supported at least two technology faculty members and a large instructional resource center. A move to a new building in the early 1980s included the purchase of a computer lab, and that lab became the center for an instructional computing course that has been a requirement for undergraduates since 1983.

One important feature of the department structure is that the technology faculty members have always been within the department and have not operated as a separate department. In recent years, the number of technology faculty members has grown to six, and all six are active members of the larger department and active participants in teacher education curriculum development. Several of the technology faculty teach teacher-education courses outside the technology area, including reading methods, educational psychology, and graduate research methods. This integration of the technology faculty into the larger teacher education program is an important part of our story.

In the early 1990s, department faculty began to include technology integration into annual department goal setting and planning. Although many faculty did not participate during the early years, all agreed to the department's emphasis on technology. The department has never required faculty participation in faculty development in technology activities. From the start, faculty participation has been voluntary. I believe that this has been an important factor in the success of our work. Although some faculty members have waited years to begin their participation in the program, faculty members have always started their work with technology based on their desire and readiness. We have faculty members who have had mentors several times since 1991 and others who asked for their first mentor as late as 2005. By 2005, however, almost every faculty member in the department has had a mentor for at least one semester. Typically, faculty members start in the mentoring program with specific instructional needs in mind. Some faculty have asked for mentors so that they can transfer their lectures to PowerPoint, while others were interested in using digital video in their teaching. One of the important features of our mentoring program is that faculty define their needs and mentors respond to these needs.

In the late 1990s the Center for Technology in Learning and Teaching (CTLT) was established in the department. Early on, the CTLT focused its research and development work on technology in teacher education. It is also important to note that the department was in the process of changing its emphasis in the late 1990s. Located in a research university, the department increased the emphasis on faculty research activity during this time. This change in emphasis was characterized by hiring new faculty with strong research records, hiring senior faculty with established research agendas, and increasing faculty time for research.

Another important piece of the story is that I became department chair in 1991. I was the first department chair from the technology faculty, and this leadership position created both challenges and opportunities for our faculty development in technology work. The major challenge was that there was a fear among some faculty that technology would be over-emphasized and over-valued in the department. Given these fears, I was very careful to begin technology initiatives slowly and to make all work in this area voluntary. Although this approach required patience, I believe that it was a significant factor in our ultimate department future with technology. Given that the department had and continued to have a committed, creative, faculty, I think it has been very important that faculty have pursued interests in using technology when and where they found it appropriate and useful.

In summary, the department is home for a relatively typical, large, teacher education program in a large public university. Characteristics that might distinguish the department include a rich history in technology integration, the placement of the technology faculty in the department, and a department chair with a technology background as well as a strong commitment to faculty autonomy. The Center for Technology in Learning and Teaching described next is also an important integrating structure relative to the department's work on integrating technology into teacher education.

THE CENTER FOR TECHNOLOGY IN LEARNING AND TEACHING

The Center for Technology in Learning and Teaching (CTLT) was established in 1996 to support and disseminate the scholarship and professional practice of knowledge, especially in the area of technology and teacher education (http://www.ctlt.iastate.edu/). More than a physical space, the CTLT is a community comprised of a collegial, collaborative group of faculty, undergraduate students, and graduate students in the Department of Curriculum and Instruction (see Figure 1.1). The Center is located in a technology-rich learning and research environment that includes six computer labs, audio and digital video production facilities, a model student-centered classroom with distance education capabilities, and equipment

Figure 1.1. Center for Technology in Learning and Teaching.

Figure 1.2. CTLT desk.

for faculty and student research (see Figure 1.2). The work of the CTLT combines research and practice on technology in teacher education.

The daily operation of the CTLT includes providing technical support for faculty and students, checking out equipment to faculty and students, managing six computer laboratories, and conducting research and development projects. Graduate and undergraduate students provide much of the leadership for the operation of the CTLT. The CTLT provides facilities, support, and a welcoming environment for faculty and students alike.

THE GOAL

From the early years of our department work, the goal for technology infusion was to use technology applications to improve the teacher education program. The vision was that technology could improve student learning in the program, and the job of the faculty was to discover and implement technology in ways that would strengthen student learning. The goal was never teaching about technology, but instead to use technology to expand and enhance our curriculum. Ultimately, the goal of the program described in this book is to change and improve faculty's use of technology in the teacher education program. Thus, the program not only helps faculty integrate instructional technologies into their teaching but also contributes to the diffusion of these technologies throughout teacher education programs.

Students learning about technology had never been a problem for this department. Having offered a required course in media (which evolved into a course in computers and technology) for two decades, the student technology knowledge piece of the program was firmly in place. In the early years, the knowledge that students were receiving a strong grounding in technology uses freed the faculty to integrate technology into their course work. The faculty was never asked to teach about the technology, only to use it effectively for student learning.

We found early in the program history that integrating technology into the teacher education curriculum was a much more difficult task than teaching and requiring the single technology course. Clearly, effective integration involves the majority of faculty in the department and involves extensive staff development work. Our department journey toward effective integration has been both slow and steady.

Over time department faculty members have developed a variety of approaches to using technology in their teaching, from web-based discussion groups to direct connections to K–12 classrooms. Applications tend to be very subject specific. While math educators have developed opportunities for students to work in groups with complex problem-solving cases and used video to help students understand learners' mathematical thinking, literacy educators have developed reading and writing activities that use technology to heighten student awareness of audience (see Figure 1.3 and Figure 1.4).

INITIAL APPROACHES

In 1991, I became chair of the department, and we began our work on infusing technology into our teacher education curriculum. Up to that

Figure 1.3. Using video to analyze and report on learners' mathematical thinking.

Figure 1.4. Using technology to develop reading and writing activities.

point, my major work with technology and learning had been with K–12 teachers. I had conducted workshops and written materials for K–12 teachers, and I had enjoyed the opportunity to work in classrooms. In about 1991, it became evident to me that I needed to focus my work on teacher education faculty since my work in K–12 indicated to me that teacher education programs needed to produce students with rich technology backgrounds. In order to do this, we needed to provide faculty with the skills and vision necessary to use technology effectively in their classes.

We began our work in the department very slowly and worked to ensure the voluntary nature of the program. In 1991, we were able to purchase computers for each of our 35 full-time faculty. This was a major change. Before that time, only a few faculty members who had grant support had computers in their offices. Although the faculty members were generally enthusiastic about the computers, several made little or no effort to use them. I recall one support staff person expressing concern to me that we had faculty who didn't even know how to turn on the machine. My reply was that we needed to be patient and work to develop a culture where faculty members would want and need to use the computers.

In the early 1990s, workshops on learning to use the computers were provided and many faculty chose to attend. We found, however, that it became increasingly difficult to schedule workshops at times when faculty could attend and that the individual faculty members had such different needs that finding topics for the workshops was problematic.

MENTORING EMERGES

After about one year of workshop activity, we decided that we needed a more individualized approach for our very individualistic faculty. It was obvious that one-on-one attention would be the best solution, but we did not have enough faculty and staff in technology to provide this level of support. Given this dilemma, we began to consider the possibility of using our graduate students as technology mentors for the faculty. Our trial run for the idea began in 1991 when I taught a Technology in Teacher Education course to about 10 graduate students. The fieldwork for the course involved working with one faculty member on technology for about one hour each week.

Faculty members were asked to sign up for a technology mentor, and then graduate student mentors were matched with faculty members. Over the years, I have come to realize that this initial matching is an important part of the success of the program. Students and faculty need to be matched on the basis of common curriculum interests and personality compatibility. The personality compatibility feature is a bit difficult to define and involves my knowledge of both the faculty and the students. It is also important that faculty with more advanced technology needs be matched with students with advanced technology knowledge. Over the years, most of our matches have been successful, but occasionally changes had to be made.

THE TECHNOLOGY IN TEACHER EDUCATION COURSE: THE COMMUNITY

All the graduate student mentors in our program are enrolled in a 2 or 3 credit course entitled Technology in Teacher Education (CI 610). The course meets for 2 hours each week, and in addition to class meetings, each student in the course mentors at least one faculty member for at least 1 hour per week.

The course provides a central community-building opportunity for the mentors. Each week, about one hour of class time is devoted to discussion of the week's experiences with faculty mentoring. In these sessions, mentors share some of the challenges of their mentoring experiences. The group often addresses technical questions emerging from the mentoring. Typically, someone in the group will have a solution for a technical challenge and/or the group will suggest a resource that could be useful.

Even more important than the technical discussions are the discussions centered on approaches and techniques that have been useful for both mentors and mentees. When one mentor describes attending a faculty

Figure 1.5. First large group meeting.

member's class so that he/she can better understand that person's teaching style, others in the group may pick up these ideas as a useful approach. When a mentor faces challenges in his/her work with a faculty member, the group enthusiastically solves the problem.

As part of the course, we always have two large group meetings of mentors and mentees. At the first meeting, typically held in the second or third week of the semester (see Figure 1.5), each mentor and mentee pair describes the goals they have set for their work together. This first large group meeting provides an opportunity to share interesting ideas. It also establishes a community of faculty and students who will be working on technology integration issues during that semester. Often, both faculty and graduate students will discover new ideas for projects and applications during these sessions.

At the end of each semester, a second large-group mentor and mentee meeting is held. This meeting is a combination report-back and celebration session (see Figure 1.6). At this time, each pair shares their major successes for the semester and their future plans for work on technology integration. This opportunity to share accomplishments has been an important part of the building of our faculty expertise in technology integration.

EFFECTS OVER TIME

As indicated earlier, our department progress in the area of technology integration has been slow and steady. After 14 years of regular mentoring programs, it is clear that the majority of the faculty in our department have made significant advances in their adoption of technology and their ability

Figure 1.6. Faculty member presenting project at second large group meeting.

to use technology to improve learning and teaching in their classes. Although progress in one semester may seem slow, progress and diffusion over time has been significant. Many faculty members in our department have participated in the mentoring program for several semesters. One reading/literacy faculty member tells of participating in the program every year for fourteen years. She now uses technology applications easily in her classes. She has web-enhanced classes, digital video cases, and direct distance education connections to K–12 classrooms. She has won grant support for her work and has published several research articles on her work with technology in reading methods classes. At a recent conference, she told her story by describing a television commercial for an SUV. This particular commercial showed an SUV that was raised by a group of sports cars and thus assumed some of the grace and ease of operation characteristic of sports cars. In her analogy, she was a faculty member who, over the years, had been influenced by a group of technology graduate students. As she said it, "Through these experiences, I am now hanging with the techies!"

The history of our program suggests the power of the mentoring experience for both faculty and students. This same history also tells us that progress will be slow and steady and that the real power of such a program is not in a one- or two-year program, but in a program that becomes institutionalized in a department or college. I have been asked why our mentoring program has not ended, given that our entire faculty has had ample opportunity to participate. One of the interesting characteristics of computers and technology, however, is that something new regularly appears and, at this time, the possibilities for developing new approaches for learning and teaching seem endless. In the early years of the program, faculty

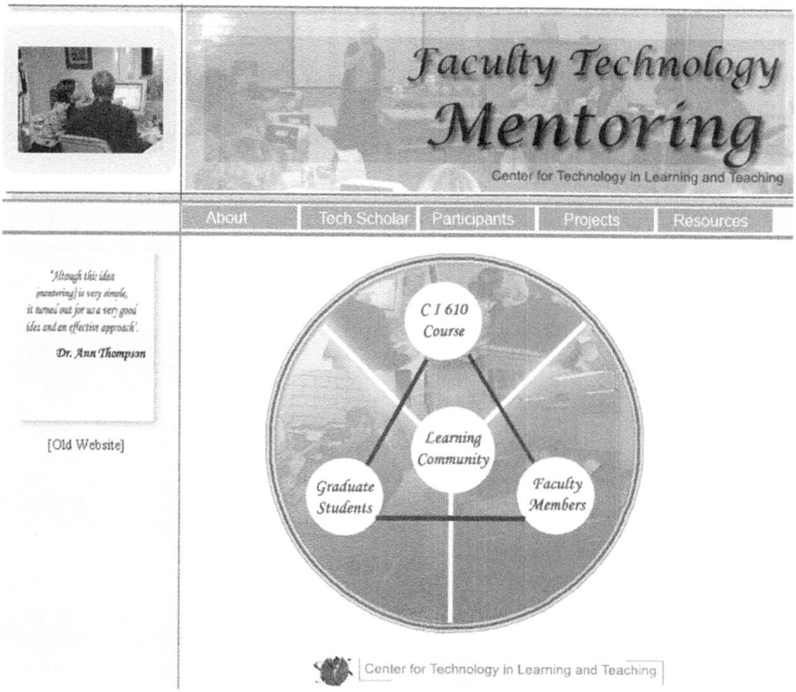

Figure 1.7. Mentoring web site.

were learning to use e-mail and tools like word processing and spreadsheets. Of late, we have focused much more on web enhancements for classes, digital video and problem based learning in simulated environments. I am confident that my description of program content in five years will be quite different once again. Although I cannot accurately project what our emphasis will be then, I believe that virtual reality environments and direct linkages to schools will be among our agenda items.

THE WEB SITE

In order to document and disseminate the faculty mentoring program described in this book, Hsueh-Hua Chuang has created a web site for the program (http://www.ci.hs.iastate.edu/mentor/homepage.html, see Figure 1.7). The site contains information about the program, mentoring cases, resources on mentoring programs, interviews with faculty and specific examples of faculty work with technology in their classes. This site provides a useful supplement to this book.

REFERENCES

November, A. (2001). *Empowering students with technology*. Arlington Heights, Illinois: Skylight Professional Development.

Rogers, E.M. (2003). *Diffusion of innovations* (5th ed.). New York, NY: Free Press.

CHAPTER 2

ROLE OF THE FACULTY MENTORING PROGRAM IN THE ADOPTION AND DIFFUSION OF INSTRUCTIONAL TECHNOLOGY

The Theoretical Perspective

Ismail Sahin

Ultimately, the faculty technology mentoring program described in this book is designed to facilitate change in faculty members' use of technology to improve instruction. The cases described in this book tell stories of both faculty adoption and diffusion of technology and we believe that Rogers' (2003) Diffusion of Innovations Theory provides the most useful theoretical lens for understanding this process. Thus, we will use Rogers' work as the primary theoretical lens for explaining how each element of the one-on-one faculty technology mentoring program contributes to encouraging the faculty adoption and diffusion. Although Rogers' theory is the main theoretical frame used throughout this book, we also find Social Learning Theory (Bandura, 1977) and the Concerns-Based Adoption Model

Faculty Mentoring: The Power of Students in Developing Technology Expertise, pages 13–27

(CBAM) (Hall & Hord, 1987) useful for explaining and interpreting our work. In Chapter 7, Pamuk uses the CBAM to describe the developing levels of concern of his faculty mentee. In this chapter, we provide an overview of Rogers' diffusion of Innovations Theory, as well as an introduction to Social Learning Theory and the Concerns-Based Adoption Theory. We then briefly suggest how these theories guide and explain some of the findings in the cases described in Chapters 4–10.

DIFFUSION OF INNOVATIONS THEORY

Researchers have argued that Rogers' Diffusion of Innovations Theory is the most appropriate model for studying the adoption of technology in higher education and educational environments (Medlin, 2001; Parisot, 1995). Thus, many research studies in areas such as political science, public health, communications, history, economics, technology, and education have used Rogers' theory as the theoretical framework in investigating the diffusion and adoption of an innovation (Dooley, 1999; Stuart, 2000) because the innovation-decision process described as "an information-seeking and information-processing activity" by Rogers provides a detailed description of the change process. For us, Rogers' theory provides a theoretical base for both describing and explaining the components of the faculty technology mentoring program. Also, it provides a foundation for understanding the role of the mentoring program in supporting faculty change.

Four Elements of Diffusion of Innovations

While adoption is the "full use of an innovation as the best course of action available" (Rogers, 2003, p. 177), diffusion is "the process in which an innovation is communicated through certain channels over time among the members of a social system" (Rogers, 2003, p. 5). The four main elements of the diffusion of innovations are innovation, communication channels, time, and social system. Innovation is defined as "an idea, practice, or project that is perceived as new by an individual or other unit of adoption" (Rogers, 2003, p. 12). For the successful adoption of an innovation, uncertainty about the disadvantages of the innovation should be reduced. Uncertainty about an innovation's consequences is an important barrier to its adoption. Thus, individuals should be aware of the advantages and consequences of the innovation to decrease the uncertainty of adopting the innovation (Rogers, 2003).

The second element of the diffusion of innovations process, communication channels, includes two types of communication: mass media and interpersonal communication. TV, radio, and newspaper serve as the mediums of mass media channels. The emphasis in our work will be on interpersonal communication channels. In fact, "diffusion is a very social process that involves interpersonal communication relationships" (Rogers, 2003, p. 19). Hence, interpersonal channels are very influential in creating and changing strong attitudes held by an individual. If these communication channels are local, that is between individuals of the social system, they become especially important in the innovation decision process (Rogers, 2003).

The other two elements of the diffusion of innovations include the time dimension and the nature of the social system. The time dimension emphasizes the fact that adoption takes place over a period time and the social system dimension emphasizes that this adoption occurs within a social system.

The Innovation-Decision Process

The innovation-decision process is composed of the following five stages: (1) knowledge, (2) persuasion, (3) decision, (4) implementation, and (5) confirmation. The innovation-decision process begins with the knowledge stage. In this step, an individual gains knowledge about the innovation and tries to determine "what the innovation is and how and why it works" (Rogers, 2003, p. 21). We know that lack of knowledge in why or how to integrate technology in the classroom is an important barrier that limits faculty use of technology in teaching (Sprague, Kopfman, & Dorsey, 1999). Hence, technology education and practice should involve both a how-to experience and a know-why knowledge experience (Seemann, 2003).

The second stage, the persuasion stage, follows the knowledge stage in the innovation-decision process and it occurs when an individual forms a negative or positive attitude toward the innovation. For Rogers (2003), the knowledge stage is more cognitive (or knowing) centered while the persuasion stage is more affective (or feeling) centered. In this stage, interpersonal communication channels are very helpful in decreasing the uncertainty about the innovation outcomes by influencing the opinions and beliefs of individuals about the innovation. "While information about a new innovation is usually available from outside experts and scientific evaluations, teachers usually seek it from trusted friends and colleagues whose subjective opinions of a new innovation are most convincing" (Sherry, 1997, p. 70).

This personal information-seeking process continues through the next stage in the adoption process, the decision stage. The idea of the adoption or rejection of the innovation is formed at the decision stage in the innovation-decision process. In this third stage, individuals prefer to try the innovation in their own situation and then reach the adoption decision. Thus, it is important that an innovation has a pilot or partial trial basis so that the innovator has the opportunity to observe the innovation in context.

At the implementation stage, individuals practice the innovation in their own context. Since "some degree of uncertainty is involved in diffusion" (Rogers, 2003, p. 6), uncertainty about the innovation outcomes in the innovator's specific context might still be an obstacle for adopting the innovation. Thus, individuals may need social reinforcements and technical assistance from others at the implementation stage, especially through interpersonal communication channels, to reduce the uncertainty about the innovation and its consequences.

The importance of interpersonal communication channels and support also continues at the confirmation stage of the innovation-decision process. Individuals look for supportive messages that confirm their decisions. At this stage, an adoption or discontinuance decision may occur based on the support for the innovation adoption and the attitude of the individual toward the innovation and its use. At the confirmation stage of adoption, the support of both administrators and peers for the implementation of the innovation is essential.

Attributes of Innovations

During the innovation decision process, adopters experience several attributes of the innovation. Rogers (2003) describes five characteristics of innovations that help to decrease uncertainty about the innovation: (1) relative advantage, (2) compatibility, (3) complexity, (4) trialability, and (5) observability. After defining the rate of adoption as "the relative speed with which an innovation is adopted by members of a social system" (Rogers, 2003, p. 221), Rogers states that "individuals' perceptions of these characteristics predict the rate of adoption of innovations" (Rogers, 2003, p. 219). Among the five attributes of innovations, relative advantage is the strongest predictor of the rate of adoption of an innovation.

Relative advantage is "the degree to which an innovation is perceived as being better than the idea it supersedes" (Rogers, 2003, p. 229). Individuals should see the value of the innovation to adopt. Compatibility is "the degree to which an innovation is perceived as consistent with the existing values, past experiences, and needs of potential adopters" (Rogers, 2003, p. 15). In contrast to the other attributes of innovations, complexity is negatively correlated with the rate of adoption. For Rogers, complexity is "the degree to which an innovation is perceived as relatively difficult to understand and use" (Rogers, 2003, p. 15). Trialability and observability are the last two attributes that are positively correlated with the rate of adoption.

According to Rogers, trialability is "the degree to which an innovation may be experimented with on a limited basis" and observability is "the degree to which the results of an innovation are visible to others" (Rogers, 2003, p. 16). The more an innovation has relative advantage, compatibility, simplicity (opposite of the complexity attribute), trialability, and observability, the faster it is adopted.

Figure 2.1 provides a visual summary of the main features of Rogers' theory. The figure shows that the process starts with the knowledge stage and ends with the confirmation of the innovation. The figure also indicates that the effects of the five attributes of the innovation are part of successful adoption. The availability of the attributes makes the adoption process faster.

In addition to Rogers' theory, Social Learning Theory (Bandura, 1977) and the Concerns-Based Adoption Model (Hall & Hord, 1987) also have some basic elements that directly relate to the role of the faculty mentoring program in the adoption and diffusion of instructional technologies in teacher education programs and K–12 schools. In Social Learning Theory, Bandura (1977) categorizes the influences on human social behavior as personal, environmental, and behavioral (Dembo, 1994; Schunk, 2000). Since personal factors such as expertise in and attitude toward an innovation are crucial in the knowledge and persuasion stages of the innovation-decision process, they can affect individuals' learning and use of the innovation.

The adoption and diffusion of an innovation occur in a social environment, so individuals also learn by observing other members of the social system and it is inevitable that environmental factors will shape this observational learning. Similarly, behavioral factors such as outcome expectation, goal setting, and self-efficacy are among the factors that affect learning (Schunk, 2000). Observational learning or modeling is a central theme in Social Learning Theory. The sub-processes of observational learning consist of attention, retention, reproduction, and motivation. These are all necessary conditions for successful vicarious learning. After paying initial attention to the innovation adoption through observing others, individuals are in position to remember and reproduce it. Motivation is a positive factor throughout the innovation diffusion process.

Similar to Rogers' theory, the Concerns-Based Adoption Model (Hall & Hord, 1987) is another popular adoption model that is used to study the process of adopting innovations (Sherry & Gibson, 2002). In this model, Hall and Hord (1987) describe eight different levels of use of an innovation: non-use, orientation, preparation, mechanical use, routine, refinement, integration, and renewal. While adopting an innovation, the user goes through the following stages of concern about the adoption: awareness, informational, personal, management, consequence, collaboration,

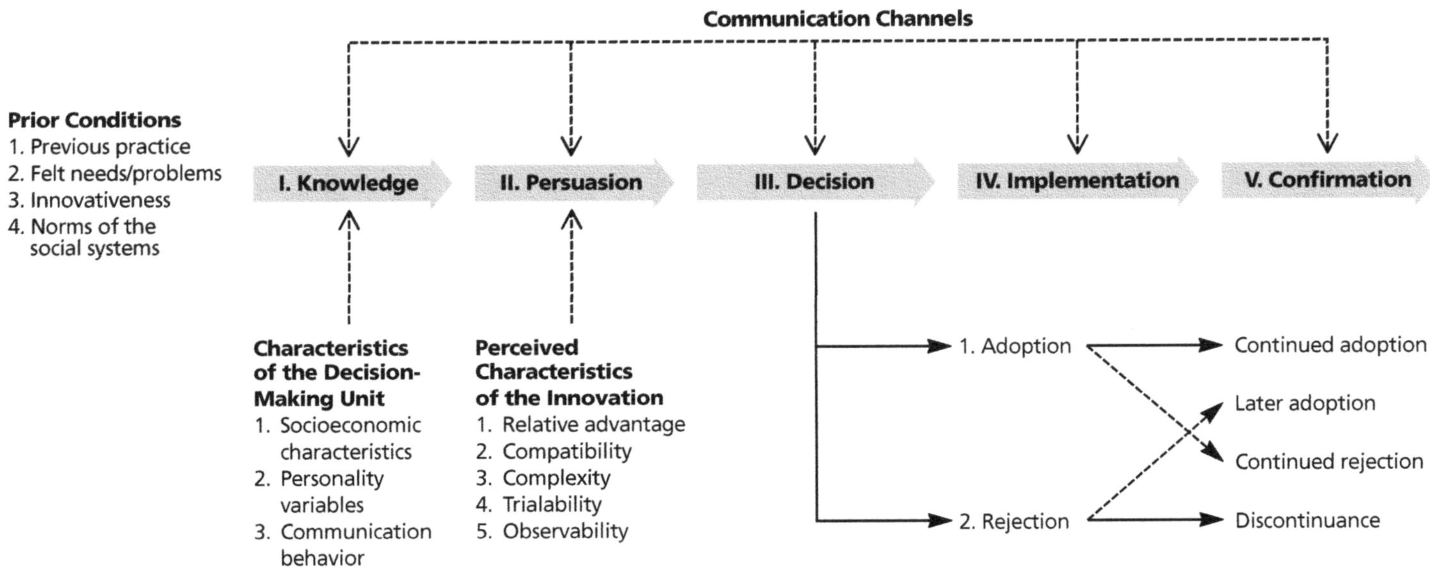

Figure 2.1. A Model of five stages in the innovation-decision process. (Source: *Diffusion of Innovations*, Fifth Edition by Everett M. Rogers. © 2003 The Free Press.)

and refocusing. While the personal and informational stages are linked to the user, the management stage is related to the task and the last three stages are connected to the impact of the innovation.

While the Concerns-Based Adoption Model focuses more on the adoption process of an innovation, Social Learning Theory deals with explaining the observational and social learning that is related to the diffusion of an innovation (see Table 2.1). However, Diffusion of Innovations Theory looks at both the adoption and the diffusion of an innovation and thus we emphasize this theory in examining both the adoption and diffusion effects of the technology mentoring program. In the next section, main components of Diffusion of Innovations Theory, along with the key elements of Social Learning Theory (Bandura, 1977) and Concerns-Based Adoption Model (Hall & Hord, 1987), will be used as a frame to describe the crucial characteristics of the one-on-one faculty technology mentoring program in the adoption and diffusion of instructional technology.

Table 2.1. Relevant Theories and Their Major Foci

Theory	*Main Contribution*	*Adoption*	*Diffusion*
Diffusion of Innovations (Rogers, 2003)	Process of adoption and diffusion of innovations	✔	✔
CBAM (Hall & Hord, 1977)	Characteristics of individual adoption and concern	✔	
Social Learning Theory (Bandura, 1977)	Observational and social learning		✔

THE ROLE OF THE FACULTY MENTORING PROGRAM IN THE ADOPTION AND DIFFUSION OF INSTRUCTIONAL TECHNOLOGY

As indicated, Rogers' (2003) theory provides the main theoretical lens to view, understand, and explain the components of the one-on-one faculty technology mentoring program. The one-on-one faculty mentoring program encourages individual faculty member's integration of instructional technologies for their teaching and contributes to the diffusion of these technologies throughout the teacher education program. Faculty members who participated as mentees in the program play a critical role in the adoption and diffusion of the technologies throughout the teacher education program. These faculty members become models and leaders for others in the area of instructional technology adoption.

Adoption of Instructional Technologies

The one-on-one faculty mentoring program provides faculty mentees with the elements of successful technology adoption. The main purpose of the innovation-decision process is to motivate individuals to reduce their uncertainty about the innovation and its outcomes. In the faculty technology mentoring program, graduate student mentors help and support faculty mentees through the steps of the innovation-decision process. Mentors help faculty members use technology for teaching and assist them in preparing their own instructional materials. Thus, the faculty technology mentoring program creates a knowledge base for faculty that is the first and most important step of the innovation-decision process. In his Social Learning Theory, Bandura (1977) describes knowledge and attitude as personal factors that affect the behaviors of individuals. The one-on-one mentoring sessions pay attention to both the knowledge and attitudes that are necessary for faculty change and development in instructional technologies. Each of the mentoring stories in this book describes the growth in knowledge about technology applications that occurs for the faculty members and teachers in the program. In Chapter 1, Thompson described the steady growth in knowledge of a reading/literacy faculty member who participated in the program every year for fourteen years, became an expert in the use of technology in her field, and used this knowledge to gain grants for her work, publish articles, and advance her teaching in reading methods classes.

The just in time, one-on-one support from mentors helps faculty members develop positive attitudes toward these technologies and these attitudes are very important at the persuasion stage of the innovation-decision process. The approach also helps to decrease their uncertainty about instructional technologies. For instance, in Chapter 4, Lindstrom will describe her efforts to lower her mentee's anxiety and frustration with instructional technology and to increase his comfort level in learning and using the technology independently. Thus, the approach described in this book contributes to the adoption of instructional technologies by providing knowledge and encouraging faculty members' positive attitudes toward these technologies that are related to the knowledge and persuasion stages that lead them to come to the decision of adopting these technologies into their teaching.

Each of the theories used in our work make it clear that it is essential for a training program to provide a trial basis for learners in instructional technologies. In the mentoring program, faculty members not only learn about the uses of instructional technologies but also practice these technologies, modify them based on their instructional needs, and apply them to their teaching methods and curriculum. Mentors support faculty mentees through the implementation stage of the innovation-decision process.

Mentors work with faculty members in their offices and also provide support and encouragement as faculty members try technology use in their classrooms. For example, in Chapters 5 and 6, Chuang and Li, respectively, will describe their roles in the implementation stage with helping their mentees practice and use different computer applications such as WebCT, Power Point, Excel, and Eudora for teaching-, research-, and administrative-related purposes. Their social reinforcements and technical assistance in instructional technologies helped faculty members practice these technologies successfully and effectively. Faculty members' successful uses of and experiences with instructional technologies reduced their uncertainty about these technologies and led them to the successful integration of instructional technologies into their teaching at the confirmation stage of the innovation-decision process. As mentioned by Chuang in Chapter 5, faculty members' positive experiences with instructional technology from the mentoring program not only helped them confirm the adoption of the technology into their academic work but also encouraged them to try new and different technology applications.

In the preface of this book, Thompson stated that many faculty members did not complete traditional staff development workshops since these programs do not meet their individual needs and expectations. Thompson suggests that general workshops do not appeal to faculty members because they do not see how many technology applications will be useful for their current needs. Because the faculty mentoring program allows faculty to define particular technology approaches they would like to learn and apply, faculty are working in areas that are important to them and to their instruction. Thus, faculty are likely to be working in areas where they can see the relative advantage of instructional technologies and we know that the relative advantage attribute is the strongest predictor of the rate of adoption of an innovation. In the one-on-one mentoring sessions, mentors emphasize how instructional technologies can be used successfully and effectively and how these technologies help faculty improve their teaching and student learning. Others have suggested that if educators see that technology has value in their specific instructional context, then they will use it (Finley, 2003; McKenzie, 2001; Parisot, 1995; Spotts, 1999).

In the Social Learning Theory (Bandura, 1977) and the Concerns-Based Adoption Model (Hall & Hord, 1987), outcome expectation and consequence, respectively, are similar terms to relative advantage. If learners think that an innovation is appropriate for them and provides them with rewarding outcomes, they will more likely adopt the innovation (Schunk, 2000). The fact that the mentoring program has always been a voluntary process for faculty relates directly to these attributes. In every case in this book, the faculty member or teacher chose to participate in the program and thus acknowledged a desire to use technology in teaching. Therefore, each faculty member enters the program with at least a partial positive outcome expectation and a sense of relative advantage.

Another motivation factor in the adoption process of instructional technology is the compatibility attribute. One of the main goals of the one-on-one faculty mentoring program is to show faculty members the applicability and appropriateness of instructional technologies for their individual teaching needs. Thus, the faculty technology mentoring program matches graduate student mentors and faculty mentees based on faculty members' prior knowledge, teaching needs, and experiences with instructional technologies in an effort to provide opportunities for the most appropriate applications for a particular faculty member's needs. As mentioned by Dr. Abelson in Chapter 4, workshops were not helpful for him because they were either "over his head or didn't have anything to do with what he needed to know". Dr. Abelson found that, in contrast, the mentoring program addressed his individual needs directly. We know that a lack of compatibility in instructional technology with individual needs may negatively affect the individual's instructional technology use (McKenzie, 2001; Sherry, 1997) and that when instructional technologies are compatible with faculty needs, then uncertainty will decrease and the rate of adoption of these technologies will increase. The faculty mentoring program described in this book seeks to provide opportunities for faculty members to define and experience compatible technology applications.

In addition to supporting compatibility, the faculty mentoring program works to minimize the complexity of the adoption process. Mentors are encouraged to carefully define faculty knowledge and needs and to provide appropriate support for learning, with an emphasis on creating a positive learning environment. By providing appropriate training and knowledge, based on the level of faculty experience with instructional technologies, graduate student mentors emphasize the simplicity of these technologies to learn and use. Faculty members in the program contrast this experience to the feeling that workshop content is way over their heads and much too complicated to use effectively. Others suggest that when faculty members see technologies as user-friendly, then they are more likely to adopt them successfully for the delivery of course materials (Martin, 2003).

One of the most significant characteristics of the faculty technology mentoring program is its focus on individual learning. As mentioned by Thompson in the preface of the book, the program pays attention to "the need for individualized one-on-one technology assistance for faculty". In fact, individual learning and use of self-directed informational sources are two significant predictors of level of instructional technology use by faculty members (Sahin & Thompson, 2005). Moreover, personal and optional innovations usually are adopted faster than the innovations involving an organizational or collective innovation-decision (Rogers, 2003). The very personal approach of the faculty mentoring program places the innovation adoption decision in the hands of the individual faculty member.

In the one-on-one mentoring sessions, faculty members have enough opportunity to learn, try, and reinvent instructional technologies for their individual purposes. Rogers described reinvention as "the degree to which an innovation is changed or modified by a user in the process of its adoption and implementation" (Rogers, 2003, p. 180). The concept of reinvention is called reproduction by Bandura (1977) in the Social Learning Theory and refocusing by Hall and Hord (1987) in the Concerns-Based Adoption Model. As the final stage of the seven, concerns about an innovation in the Concerns-Based Adoption Model, reinvention (or refocusing) confirms the successful adoption of the innovation by the user. The more reinvention occurs, the more rapidly an innovation is adopted and becomes institutionalized. In Chapters 9 and 10, Babcock and Johnson, respectively, will tell us that the one-on-one mentoring sessions helped their mentees become confident in instructional technologies, and eventually the mentees started to use and modify these technologies for their own needs without help. Many of the mentoring stories in this book indicate that the faculty technology mentoring program provides faculty members with an active and effective individual learning environment that involves an adequate amount of trialability.

The last attribute of innovations according to Rogers is observability. Similar to relative advantage, compatibility, and trialability, observability is also positively correlated with the rate of adoption of an innovation. Observational learning is also an important part of Social Learning Theory and goal setting is one of the key factors that affect learning (Schunk, 2000). The observational learning environment in the mentoring program fits with the elements of Social Learning Theory in that it meets faculty interests and expectations by providing them with a permanent, productive, and motivational learning environment. In Chapters 8, 9, and 10, the reader will see that the collaborative partnership between the mentors and their mentees creates a successful observational learning environment for them and that lists of goals established based on the mentees' needs contribute to this learning. In the faculty technology mentoring program, faculty members have opportunities to observe the uses of instructional technologies by both graduate student mentors and other faculty members. In the weekly one-on-one mentoring sessions and the group meetings, involving all the mentors and mentees, faculty members actually see concrete examples of innovative and meaningful uses of instructional technologies. Having the opportunity to observe these examples creates a positive environment for technology adoption and a learning environment where faculty members are likely to share their own technology uses. The opportunity for faculty members to both share and observe successful technology applications creates an ideal environment for the diffusion of instructional technologies throughout a teacher education program.

Diffusion of Instructional Technologies

In both Diffusion of Innovation Theory and Social Learning Theory, social environment is an important factor in behavioral change. These theories highlight the importance of vicarious learning that supports this change by providing interpersonal channels. The one-on-one faculty mentoring program not only helps faculty members adopt instructional technologies but also uses interpersonal communication channels to diffuse these technologies throughout the teacher education program. In our work, we have observed a similar phenomenon in K–12 environments. Kouadio and Babcock in Chapters 8 and 9 will show the importance of collegial learning and collaboration in the diffusion of instructional technologies in K–12 school settings. In both teacher education and K–12 environments, collegial interactions serve as interpersonal channels that are very influential, especially through the persuasion, decision, and confirmation stages of the innovation-decision process. In both environments, close peers' subjective evaluations of the innovation are powerful in reducing uncertainty about the innovation outcomes (Rogers, 2003; Sherry, 1997). Faculty members who participated in the faculty technology mentoring program encourage and help other faculty members to have positive attitudes toward instructional technologies by showing the successful adoption of these technologies into their teaching. As mentioned in the last chapter of this book, the large group meetings gathering all mentors and mentees of the mentoring program provide faculty members with the opportunity to share their experiences and concrete technology applications with other faculty members. Throughout this book, the reader will see examples of the participants in the mentoring program supporting their colleagues through the stages of the innovation-decision process and reducing their colleagues' uncertainty about instructional technologies and their consequences.

For instance, in Chapter 8, Kouadio will mention that the mentoring program was helpful for her and her mentee in modeling the advantages of computer technology to their students and colleagues. In fact, collegial interaction and communication is a significant predictor of instructional technology use by faculty members (Sahin & Thompson, 2005). Literature has also emphasized the importance of collegial interaction and support in predicting and encouraging the faculty adoption of technology (Casmar, 2001; Hagenson, 2001; Hoerup, 2001; Stoik, 2001; Surendra, 2001). This collegial communication is also helpful to show the relative advantage, compatibility, simplicity, trialability, and observability of instructional technologies.

Since role modeling (or peer observation) is a key motivational factor in the adoption and diffusion of technology (Parisot, 1995), the successful and effective uses of instructional technologies by faculty members who participated in the faculty technology mentoring program provide the opportunity to show their colleagues that instructional technologies provide many advantages and opportunities for them to meet their instructional needs and that these technologies are applicable and appropriate to their teaching methods and strategies. In Chapters 8 and 9, the reader will see that effective uses of instructional technologies by mentor and mentee teachers encouraged other K–12 teachers by showing the relative advantage and compatibility attributes of these technologies. After other faculty members observe the exemplary uses of instructional technologies by the participants of the faculty technology mentoring program and perceive these technologies as easy to learn and use, they are more likely to try and adopt these technologies into their own instruction. One faculty member made this phenomenon quite clear when she commented on another faculty member's use of video cases in instruction: "You know, if Marcia can do it, I think I can too!" Collegial interaction and modeling provide a social reinforcement for faculty change and development in the uses of instructional technologies.

CONCLUSION

The one-on-one faculty technology mentoring program described in this book has played a key role in the adoption and diffusion of instructional technology in our teacher education program. Elements of the program are based in Diffusion of Innovations Theory (Rogers, 2003), along with major components of Social Learning Theory (Bandura, 1977) and the Concerns-Based Adoption Model (Hall & Hord, 1987). The faculty technology mentoring program helps and supports faculty members through all the stages (knowledge, persuasion, decision, implementation, and confirmation) of the innovation-decision process. This program also emphasizes the five characteristics (relative advantage, compatibility, simplicity, trialability, and observability) of innovations that influence faculty members' likelihood of adopting a new technology into their teaching (Anderson, Varnhagen, & Campbell, 1998; Bennett & Bennett, 2003; Parisot, 1995; Slyke, 1998; Surendra, 2001) Finally, the emphasis of the one-on-one faculty technology mentoring program on collegial communication and interaction works to expand individual adoption into diffusion of instructional technologies successfully throughout teacher education programs and K–12 environments.

REFERENCES

Anderson, T., Varnhagen, S., & Campbell, K. (1998). Faculty adoption of teaching and learning technologies: Contrasting earlier adopters and mainstream faculty. *The Canadian Journal of Higher Education, 28*(23), 71–78.

Bandura, A. (1977). *Social learning theory.* Englewood Cliffs, NJ: Prentice Hall.

Bennett, J., & Bennett, L. (2003). A review of factors that influence the diffusion of innovation when structuring a faculty training program. *Internet and Higher Education, 6,* 53–63.

Casmar, S. P. (2001). The adoption of computer technology by faculty in a college of education: an analysis of administrative planning issues (Doctoral dissertation, Washington State University, 2001). *ProQuest DigitalDissertations.* (UMI No. AAT 3025011).

Dembo, M.H. (1994). *Applying educational psychology* (5th ed.). New York, NY: Longman.

Dooley, K.E. (1999). Towards a holistic model for the diffusion of educational technologies: An integrative review of educational innovation studies. *Educational Technology & Society 2*(4), 35–45.

Finley, T.R. (2003). A descriptive study of utilization of technology from a perspective of full-time faculty in Virginia's higher education teacher-education programs (Doctoral dissertation, The George Washington University, 2003). *ProQuest DigitalDissertations.* (UMI No. AAT 3083800).

Hagenson, L. (2001). The integration of technology into teaching by university college of education faculty (Master thesis, Oklahoma State University, 2001).

Hall, G.E., & Hord, S.M. (1987). *Change in schools: Facilitating the process.* New York, NY: State University of New York Press.

Hoerup, S.L. (2001). Diffusion of an innovation: Computer technology integration and the role of collaboration (Doctoral dissertation, Virginia Polytechnic Institute and State University, 2001). *ProQuest DigitalDissertations.* (UMI No. AAT 3031436).

Martin, M.H. (2003). Factors influencing faculty adoption of Web-based courses in teacher education programs within the State University of New York (Doctoral dissertation, Virginia Polytechnic Institute and State University, 2001). *ProQuest Digital Dissertations.* (UMI No. AAT 3089087).

McKenzie, J. (2001). How teachers learn technology best. *From Now On: The Educational Technology Journal, 10*(6). Retrieved March 01, 2005, from http://www.fno.org/mar01/howlearn.html

Medlin, B.D. (2001). The factors that may influence a faculty member's decision to adopt electronic technologies in instruction (Doctoral dissertation, Virginia Polytechnic Institute and State University, 2001). *ProQuest DigitalDissertations.* (UMI No. AAT 3095210).

Parisot, A.H. (1995). Technology and teaching: The adoption and diffusion of technological innovations by a community college faculty (Doctoral dissertation, Montana State University, 1995). *ProQuest DigitalDissertations.* (UMI No. AAT 9542260).

Rogers, E.M. (2003). *Diffusion of innovations* (5th ed.). New York, NY: Free Press.

Sahin, I., & Thompson, A. (2005). *Understanding faculty use of technology with the Learning/Adoption Trajectory Model.* Unpublished manuscript.

Schunk, D.H. (2000). *Learning theories: An educational perspective* (3rd ed.). Upper Saddle River, NJ: Prentice-Hall.

Seemann, K. (2003). Basic principles in holistic technology education. *Journal of Technology Education, 14*(2), 28–39.

Sherry, L. (1997). The boulder valley Internet project: Lessons learned. *THE (Technological Horizons in Education) Journal, 25*(2), 68–73.

Sherry, L., & Gibson, D. (2002). The path to teacher leadership in educational technology. *Contemporary Issues in Technology and Teacher Education* [Online serial], *2*(2).

Slyke, C.V. (1998). Technology cluster innovations: impacts of adding a technology to an existing cluster (Doctoral dissertation, University of South Florida, 1998). *ProQuest DigitalDissertations.* (UMI No. AAT 9911422).

Spotts, T.H. (1999). Discriminating factors in faculty use of instructional technology in higher education. *Educational Technology & Society, 2*(4), 92–99.

Sprague, D., Kopfman, K., & Dorsey, S. (1999). Faculty development in the integration of technology in teacher education courses. *Journal of Computing in Teacher Education, 14*(2), 24–28.

Stoik, J.H. (2001). Technology's role in collaboration. *Community College Journal of Research and Practice, 25*(1), 37–46.

Stuart, W.D. (2000). Influence of sources of communication, user characteristics and innovation characteristics on adoption of a communication technology (Doctoral dissertation, The University of Kansas, 2000). *ProQuest DigitalDissertations.* (UMI No. AAT 9998114).

Surendra, S.S. (2001). Acceptance of Web technology-based education by professors and administrators of a college of applied arts and technology in Ontario (Doctoral dissertation, University of Toronto, 2001). *ProQuest DigitalDissertations.* (UMI No. AAT NQ58603).

CHAPTER 3

FACULTY TECHNOLOGY MENTORING PROGRAMS

Major Trends in the Literature

Hsueh-Hua Chuang and Denise Schmidt

Some research in the field of technology in teacher education examines the effects of computer access and usage (Albion, 2001; Dougherty, 2000; Farenga & Joyce, 1996), while other studies investigate the current status of technology use in teacher education (Laffey & Musser, 1998; Maushak, Kelley, & Blodgett, 2001; OTA, 1995). A number of studies report on efforts to infuse technology across teacher education curriculum or provide diffusion of technology innovation models (Strudler & Wetzel, 1999; Strudler, Archambault, Bendixen, Anderson, & Weiss, 2003; Stuhlman, 1998; Thompson, Schmidt, & Davis, 2003). One common theme from these research findings is that, despite the availability of computers, the teacher education faculty is in need of comprehensive planning, professional development, and follow-up support to realize the vision of widespread technology integration. However, few teacher education programs have faculty who are modeling instructional methods that integrate computer technology in the classrooms (Carlson & Gooden, 1999; OTA, 1995), even though many teacher education institutions have identified the need for faculty development in the area of technology use and integration (Cavanaugh, 2002; Sprague, Kopfman, & Dorsey, 1998). In recent years, a

Faculty Mentoring: The Power of Students in Developing Technology Expertise, pages 29–46

mix of training activities, approaches, and strategies of faculty development programs to encourage faculty to learn how to integrate technology into teaching and learning is echoed in most of the PT3 (Preparing Tomorrow's Teachers to Use Technology) grant project proposals. Those approaches included committed leadership from the administration, group workshops and one-on-one technology support from technology staff as well as undergraduate and graduate students (PT3, 2004).

Several research studies have specifically identified the potential barriers involved for the faculty to begin using computer-related technology. The obstacles included lack of knowledge about software and hardware, limited visions of technology integration, schedule conflicts, and lack of administrative support (Dusick, 1998; O'Bannon, Matthew, & Thomas, 1998; OTA, 1995; Sandholtz, 2001). The removal of these obstacles would facilitate the adoption of technology diffusion in teacher education programs and thus would help teacher educators provide appropriate modeling of technology integration in their teacher preparation courses for preservice teachers.

Growing out of an urgent need for faculty to model effective technology integration in teacher education, several institutions have adopted one-on-one technology mentoring programs to better meet the specific needs of each faculty member. The one-on-one technology mentoring programs are designed to address some of the barriers associated with teacher education faculty adoption of instructional technology. The one-on-one approach motivates most faculty to learn and use instructional technologies in a nonthreatening situation and thus creates a knowledge base for the faculty in the innovation-decision process (Rogers, 2003). Typically, this unique type of just-in-time support helps faculty members develop positive attitudes toward technology use and integration in their teacher preparation courses. They could easily reach the decision stage once they are persuaded about the relative advantages of the instructional technologies. One-on-one mentoring programs also emphasize using technology in meaningful contexts in classrooms; as a result, faculty can easily experience the implementation of the instructional technologies in teaching and learning. Then faculty could reach the confirmation stage in the innovation decision process (Rogers, 2003) with the one-on-one support to reduce complexity as the approach caters more to each individual faculty member's needs. Research on faculty technology development has shown that one-shot workshops without ongoing individual technology support often fail to meet the specific needs of most educators (Sprague et al., 1998). Meanwhile, one-on-one technology mentoring models show promising results on faculty professional development in terms of developing technology integrated curriculum (Beisser, 2000; Thompson, Hansen, & Reinhart, 1996).

This chapter summarizes the literature on technology mentoring models used in higher education and K–12 schools. In addition, it identifies similarities between the models and themes that are emerging from the research on these models. Another goal of this chapter is to highlight the key elements in successful mentoring programs.

MODELS OF MENTORING PROGRAMS

Based on the need for faculty to model technology use, more teacher education programs are searching for appropriate, high-quality, professional development models. Several higher education institutions developed one-on-one mentoring models that pair faculty members with students. These mentoring models vary somewhat, based on the technology integration philosophy of the teacher education program involved. One model offered multiple, intensive training sessions through guided lessons on particular software packages followed by one-on-one mentoring support. Another model included a graduate or undergraduate course in which the fieldwork assignment paired students with faculty members interested in using technology in their courses. This mentoring model is often extended to the K–12 environment, with a focus on overcoming barriers to technology use in K–12 classrooms. In almost all of these models, a younger person served as the mentor as opposed to the traditional "hierarchical transfer of knowledge and information from an older, more experienced person to a younger, less experienced person" (Zachary, 2001, p. 1).

A variety of mentoring models are described in the sections that follow to provide an overview of mentoring staff development options. The mentoring relationship provides professional development support along with opportunities to model technology integration throughout the curriculum.

Graduate Students as Mentors

Iowa State University's Department of Curriculum and Instruction developed a mentoring model that involves graduate students as mentors through the course "Technology and Teacher Education." For the field component of this course, each graduate student is paired with a faculty member. The pairs spend approximately one hour per week working on technology-related learning tasks. This model provides an individualized approach to professional development, because each faculty member chooses the focus of the sessions based on his or her specific needs (Zachariades & Roberts, 1995). Each faculty member receives one-on-one attention to facilitate the process of technology integration. The pairing, in most cases, became a true partnership and collaboration (Stewart, 1999; Thompson et al., 1996). The course instructor organizes the mentoring program by scheduling weekly seminars in which student mentors exchange experiences, solutions, and pedagogical thoughts. This model is highly sustainable because the course is offered regularly as part of a graduate program.

In addition, with PT3 grant funding, a TechCo project was initiated in 1999 at Iowa State University. TechCo (Technology Collaboratives for Simultaneous Renewal in Teacher Education Project) is aimed to create technology-based learning experiences in a teacher education program and in collaborating K–6 schools. Several of TechCo project's goals were addressed through the implementation of a technology scholar program, which differs from the faculty one-on-one technology mentoring program described in Chapter 1 and in the cases in Chapters 4–10. Beginning in the summer of 2000, six faculty members in the Department of Curriculum and Instruction at Iowa State University applied for and were named technology scholars. The technology scholars' program, as part of the TechCo project, provided faculty members with a computer and summer salary (or a course release) to study and work one-one-one with a graduate student technology mentor to begin developing materials and ideas for integrating technology into courses that the TechCo undergraduate students would take the next year. The results from the ISU technology scholar program indicate that faculty involved in the program were motivated to work on curriculum focused and technology integrated course designs because they were given the time and one-on-one support. Faculty also expressed a willingness to continue learning about integrating technology into courses (Thompson et al., 2003).

The Graduate School of Education at George Mason University offers a similar course in their instructional technology program. Before beginning their mentoring experience, graduate students enroll in the "Faculty Development in Instructional Technology" course. Efforts are made to pair the technology abilities of students with the skills faculty want to learn. Graduate students work with faculty members to address technology anxiety and skills and to develop materials to be used in courses. Frequently, more than one semester of assistance was needed in order to reach established goals. Faculty members expressed a strong interest in participating in this project, so plans were made to connect one-on-one mentoring with an existing course (Sprague, Kopfman & Dorsey, 1998).

New Mexico State University College of Education initiated a pilot mentoring program for faculty in 1996. Five volunteer faculty members and five graduate students were matched by area of interest and technology expertise. Students met with their faculty mentees and received graduate credits as part of an internship course. Graduate students also met with the project director every other week to investigate software and solutions to faculty's questions (Gonzales et al., 1997; Gonzales & Thompson, 1998).

Instead of offering course credits, the University of New Mexico's College of Education hired graduate students as Tech Guides to provide one-on-one support in helping faculty gain computer knowledge and skills. In addition, these Tech Guides were available to present technology integration lessons in methods courses. Each Tech Guide was assigned five faculty members and worked intensively with them on an individual basis one or two hours per week. Results indicated that faculty members increased their technology skills and integrated more technology in their courses with the support of the Tech Guides (Bramble, 2000).

In another mentoring program, special education graduate students served as technology mentors as a part of their graduate assistantship in a large mid-western university. This model featured a combination of multiple training sessions and one-on-one mentoring activities to support faculty use of technology in teaching and professional development. Nineteen faculty members and nine graduate students participated in the eight-week pilot program. Graduate students attended two sessions of intensive training on using PowerPoint before they began their mentoring activities. The first session introduced the graduate students to the software program. The second session featured the PowerPoint learning packet, which the graduate students were to use with the faculty as guided practice. Faculty members also participated in a group training session, which featured PowerPoint capabilities and the learning packet. Using the scripted lessons in the learning packet as guidelines in the one-one-one mentoring activities that followed, student mentors worked with faculty members in their own offices using their own computers (Smith & O'Bannon, 1999).

Through a PT3 grant, the University of Hawaii College of Education used the Technology Intensive Course Model to successfully redesign over one third of its courses to increase both students' and faculty's use of technology. The first phase of the model used a number of strategies to recruit about 48 faculty to the project. The second phase involved having graduate student mentors from the Educational Technology Department offer one-on-one mentoring to assist faculty while designing technology-integrated curriculum. Student technology mentors were required to participate in training prior to their mentoring work. The training topics included technology intensive standards and guidelines, customer service, specific hardware and software, and role-plays to discuss solutions for a variety of situations in one-on-one mentoring sessions. Typically, the mentor/mentee pair met on a weekly basis for about an hour in the faculty mentee's office. The mentoring process started with a technology skill survey to assess the technology needs and confidence levels of the faculty mentees. Then the mentoring pair met to discuss course content and the faculty mentee's goals for redesigning the course to integrate technology. The student mentors not only provided technology support but instructional design knowledge to help the faculty mentees organize and redesign the course (Rivers, Eichelberger, & Ho, 2005).

Similar approaches can be found in other PT3 projects. For example, at the University of Northern Colorado (UNC), several of their PT3 project initiatives are to model the appropriate use of technology in UNC courses. Faculty members who were chosen to participate in the project were released from one course and were offered a budget to purchase necessary software. Then faculty were paired with an advanced student in educational technology who provided one-on-one assistance in technology support and instructional design (Javeri & Hunt, 2002). Another similar example is part of the California State University, San Bernardino PT3 project. It involved delivering multiple forms of technology training to faculty in the College of Education. One part of this training program included a mentoring model where educational technology graduate students served as mentors to faculty mentees (Leh, 2005). At Mercyhurst College, instead of recruiting technology savvy graduate students as mentors, they hired students with a strong pedagogical background who were willing to learn and work together with the faculty to integrate technology use in the classroom (Kennihan, Schaefer, & Hembrow Snyder, 2004).

UNDERGRADUATE STUDENTS AS MENTORS

Not all colleges and universities offer graduate programs in technology, so the use of undergraduate students as technology mentors is a viable option for some institutions (Beisser, Kurth, & Reinhart, 1997). The mentoring models described in this section feature undergraduate students working closely with faculty or K–12 in-service teachers.

The University of North Texas used their PT3 Capacity Building Grant to provide technology integration mentoring during the spring of 2000. A new course "Technology Integration Mentoring" required undergraduate students to work one-on-one with in-service teachers in an authentic classroom environment. In this model, undergraduate students met face-to-face three times during the semester and communicated regularly via a class listserv. The class created a web-site with resource links to technology and curriculum. The students spent the rest of the class time in classrooms paired with in-service teachers, selected personally or arranged by the instructor. The final class meeting featured presentations by the undergraduate students illustrating their collaborative work with the in-service teachers. A successful outcome from this model was the impact the two-way mentoring experience had on the undergraduate students' development as teachers. The undergraduate students served as the technology experts, but they also learned classroom management and curriculum from in-service teachers (Tyler-Wood et al., 2000).

Carson-Newman College Teacher Education Department started a mentoring program using elementary and secondary education undergraduate students to mentor faculty. This model consisted of four stages:

1. large group planning sessions,
2. small technical sessions,
3. one-on-one mentoring sessions, and
4. a final large group session for project sharing.

Requirements for the one-hour course included thirty-five hours in planning and implementing large and small group sessions, as well as preparing for and meeting in one-on-one sessions with faculty. Faculty agreed to allocate time to meet with mentors, to share projects with other faculty, and to participate in an evaluative interview. This mentoring program featured one-on-one relationships, mentoring technique training, communication with the program director, and formal commitments by both student mentors and faculty mentees (Milligan & Robinson, 2000).

In Canada, the University of Regina's Faculty of Education initiated a reciprocal mentoring model in which education students with technology expertise organized workshops for faculty members and provided one-on-one assistance following the workshops. As reciprocal mentors, faculty and students learned from each other by utilizing the students' technology skills and the pedagogical expertise of the faculty (Browne, Maeers, & Cooper, 2000).

MODELS EXTENDED TO K–12 ENVIRONMENT

According to Dwyer (1998), frequent, well planned, and collaborative activities, which are conducted in the form of on-the-job mentoring, have the potential to facilitate structural change in school environments and to transform school cultures. Several mentoring models have extended into K–12 schools by establishing innovative mentor/mentee relationships between university and K–12 school personnel.

Recognizing the need for support for successful technology use in K–12 schools, the University of Maryland collaborated with the Prince George's County Public Schools to establish a computer mentoring program. University and school personnel designed the program to prepare experienced computer-using teachers to serve as mentors for other teachers in their own schools. In this case, the university offered a course "Leadership in Computer Applications" to in-service teachers who wished to serve as mentors. Each mentor worked with one to five colleagues. In addition to formal sessions, mentors were available informally because they were teaching in the same school. The purpose of this program was to increase technology use in the curriculum and to establish sustainable collegial relationships in K–12 environments (MacArthur et al., 1995).

Franklin, Turner, Kariuki, and Duran (2001) present another mentoring model that encourages collaborative efforts between higher education and K–12 schools. This partnership between a university and an elementary school focuses on implementing strategies that address barriers to using technology in schools. Pairing instructional technology graduate students with elementary school teachers led to the sharing of technology expertise and ideas for technology integration in the existing K–12 curriculum. This mentoring model provides a cost-effective way to provide professional development for teachers who have difficulty obtaining technology support. Similarly, the Modeling Instruction with Modern Information and Communications Technologies (MIMIC) project at Cleveland State University was funded through a PT3 grant. The MIMIC project focuses on faculty development using a mentoring program that extends to K–12 environments where classroom teachers are the mentors and faculty members are the mentees (Stahlman, Nasara, & Abate, 2002).

SECONDARY SCHOOL STUDENTS AS MENTORS

The well-known Generation Y mentoring model originated in the Olympia School District in Washington, in 1996. It features an extensive involvement of students as collaborative partners with their teachers. As the project title indicates, Generation Y focuses on the generation of young people who use their technology expertise to help teachers bring technology into the classroom. In the process, students develop leadership skills and often receive recognition for their work with technology in the larger community. This program includes an instructional component for secondary students in grades 8–12. During the 18 week course, students study technology, collaboration, and project development. Students who successfully complete the course serve as mentors to teachers in extensive and authentic situations during the regular school day. They support their teachers in the integration of technology into curriculum-based projects and lesson plans. The students often maintain school networks and equipment. Schools across the nation have replicated this student mentoring model (Generation www.Y, 2001).

The University of Texas at Austin conducted project CIRCLE (Collaborative Information Resources Computer-supported Learning Environments) in collaboration with the Austin Independent School District and the Eanes Independent School District. This project used technology network tools to establish an on-line learning alliance within high schools and to explore innovative constructivist uses of technology in the classroom. A virtual learning community based on the constructivist model of learning was established between project schools and the university for collaborative and intellectual work. Teachers and selected students attended training sessions on the use of specific collaborative learning tools. These teachers and students then served as on-site technology mentors for other teachers and fellow students. The findings indicate that student mentors can be an effective technology resource and support system for teachers who are implementing new technology tools and applications (Resta, 1998).

SUMMARY OF MENTORING MODELS

Educational institutions adopted different mentoring models based on the identified needs of the teacher education programs or K–12 schools to increase technology skills and enhance technology integration. Some models includes one technology course where students are paired with faculty members who are interested in using technology in their courses. Some were pilot programs designed to match graduate or undergraduate students with faculty members or in-service teachers in a reciprocal mentoring relationship. Others offer a combination of multiple training sessions and one-on-one mentoring activities.

THEMES FROM RESEARCH ON MENTORING PROGRAMS

Several elements of successful technology mentoring models clearly emerged from a careful review of the literature. These elements included providing visions for the use of technology in teaching and learning, individualizing technology support, breaking down hierarchical structure, establishing open dialogue and collaborative relationships, providing mutual benefits for mentors and mentees, and establishing learning communities. The presence of these elements is critical in establishing and maintaining successful mentoring programs.

Providing Visions for Technology Use

Educational change is difficult to achieve, in spite of many attempts. The beliefs of educators have either assisted the change in practice or inhibited innovation (Schuttloffel, 2000). According to Papert (1980), technology provides the visionary reform in all levels of educational institutions. However, such educational reform does not occur by using one-size-fits-all models of professional development, especially when it comes to technology integration. In the one-on-one mentoring programs described in the literature, collaborative efforts among participants resulted in shared visions and more successful technology integration. Most faculty or in-service teacher mentees in these programs indicated that they developed a deeper level of understanding and a higher level of confidence in the use of technology. One teacher mentee stated:

> I think I have more confidence about managing it all now. I had ideas about using the technology but this has given me an opportunity to see the graduate student at work with the students, so I know it can be done . . . even with my class. (Franklin et al., 2001, p. 28)

This in turn strengthened "their personal and teaching related use of computers, attitudes toward educational computing, and interest in learning more about educational technology" (Generation www.Y, 2000, Executive Summary, p. 14). One faculty mentee in the School of Education at New Mexico State University mentioned:

> I began as what can be referred to as a "technophobe," but I was lucky to receive encouragement and support from technology professionals. I started using computer technology as a word processor I began to move more rapidly across the bridge from personal use to uses of technology for teaching reading. (Gonzales & Thompson, 1998, p. 167)

At the University of Hawaii, the ultimate outcome of the graduate student-faculty mentoring sessions in their PT3 grant project was a course proposal that included revised course objectives aligned to technology standards. These course proposals highlighted new instructional strategies and activities that faculty were using in their courses and specifically described ways faculty were modeling technology use in courses. From the project evaluation, the faculty reported that the one-on-one mentoring sessions were the most effective in helping them with developing technology-integrated curriculum. One faculty member with little technology experience redesigned her course and as a result required students to create electronic portfolios (Rivers, Eichelberger, & Ho, 2005). As their confidence increases, participants in these technology mentoring programs rapidly develop a vision for how to use technology in their courses and classrooms.

Individualizing Technology Support

"Teaching must start where the learner is" (Hunt, 1961, p. 268). One-on-one mentoring addresses the unique learning curve of mentees, especially with respect to technology. This model offers individualized technology support that is usually provided on site. Because each content area often required its own creative way to integrate technology into its curricula, it was difficult to provide specific content integration ideas in large group workshop sessions. Moreover, one-on-one mentoring programs allow mentees to work at their own pace. One strength of the one-on-one mentoring program at Iowa State University is the opportunity for graduate student mentors to address specific needs of faculty mentees in their own areas of interest and pedagogical beliefs (Thompson et al., 1996). The student mentors devised instruction to fit the learning styles, the skill levels, and personal interests of the faculty mentees. As one mentee indicated:

> Importantly, our one-to-one mentorship provided a risk-free atmosphere to ask rudimentary questions about files, folders, menu bars, and how an application works. Eventually, he [student mentor] introduced more complex productivity tools to present and organize information, in particular, those which would relate to my social studies methods course (Beisser et al., 1997, p. 4).

Faculty members typically like the fact that they received one-on-one support because their technology needs are addressed individually and directly. A number of the PT3 grant projects included one-on-one technology mentoring programs that addressed individual faculty needs and provided additional faculty development options. At the University of Northern Colorado, their PT3 mentoring program provided time and support for faculty members from various disciplines and with different technology background experiences to redesign their courses. Thus, faculty designed and infused technology components into their courses based on their own content area focus and needs (Javeri & Hunt, 2002). As Sahin mentioned in Chapter 2, the faculty technology program allows faculty to see the relative advantage of instructional technologies and is the first attribute of innovations according to Rogers's theory (2003), and the strongest predictor of the rate of adoption of an innovation. Faculty members found that the individual approach of the mentoring program allowed them to identify technology uses that fit their particular needs.

Breaking Down Hierarchical Structure

One-on-one mentoring models erase the traditional hierarchy in which leadership comes from above. A shared sense of common goals, opportunity, motivation, and reward between the mentor and the mentee was the prevailing mentoring paradigm in these cases, instead of a top down, one-way approach. Because of the change in the hierarchy, student mentors felt comfortable approaching faculty members with comments and worked closely with faculty to solve problems, share knowledge and gain expertise. Findings from the PT3 grant project at California State University, San Bernardino indicate that the success of their one-on-one mentoring sessions is attributed to building a trust-based relationship between student mentors and faculty mentees (Piller, Baek, & Leh, 2003). In many cases, mentors and mentees are able to "form not only a professional but a personal friendship, too" (Beisser et al., 1997, p. 325).

These technology mentoring models, unlike traditional models in which mentors usually have absolute authority (Philips-Jones, 1982), focus on collaborative efforts. Technology, as a facilitator of hierarchical change, moved institutions or schools toward a learning community to "involve students as co-creators and co-owners of the curriculum, who bring needed skills and resources to the table" (Generation www.Y, 2000, p. 13).

Establishing an Open Dialogue and Collaborative Relationships

The research indicated that mentoring is a dynamic and interactive experience. One-on-one mentoring promoted collaboration among mentors and mentees as they worked to integrate technology into courses. Case studies in mentoring programs emphasize the need for an open dialogue with both mentor and mentee expressing their feelings, knowledge, and expectations. In some models, mentors and mentees started with a formal needs assessment like the "Individual Mentoring Plan" (MacArthur et al., 1995, p. 50) or a technology skill survey (Rivers et al., 2005). In other models, the mentoring pairs wrote a less formal set of goals (Gonzales et al., 1997; Sprague et al., 1998; Thompson et al., 1996) or they collaborated on outlining a course proposal (Rivers et al., 2005). A mutual respect and trust developed during the mentoring process as the mentor and mentee worked collaboratively to integrate technology into curricula. This kind of partnership often resulted in collaborative projects. In the University of North Texas model, preservice teachers (the mentors) showcased their work with classroom teachers (the mentees) in their final face-to-face class meeting (Tyler-Wood, Christensen, Arrowood, Allen, & Maldonado., 2000).

Providing Mutual Benefits

Many mentoring models are set up as a reciprocal relationship in which the faculty mentee learned about integrating technology into their courses and the student mentor learned from the pedagogical expertise in a certain field. Because of the dynamic nature of the mentoring process, the roles of student mentors gradually change and evolve. Therefore, the benefits for education students as mentors include the opportunity to establish connections with faculty members, to learn from the faculty members' pedagogical expertise, and to understand more clearly how faculty members successfully integrate technology into their courses. The faculty mentees increased their ability to visualize and conceptualize technology use in the classroom through the brainstorming process with their mentors (Beisser, 2000; Browne et al., 2000; Gonzales et al., 1997; Sprague et al., 1998; Stewart, 1999; Thompson et al., 1996).

In K–12 environments, student mentors and teachers benefit from "an authentic, multidisciplinary, project-based experience of doing valuable work . . . teachers receive individualized support for integrating technology in their particular classroom" (Generation www.Y, 2000, p. 13). In addition, students gain leadership and communication skills through this authentic learning environment. In project CIRCLE, teachers indicated that one of the important benefits for student mentors was the improved behavior and boost of self-esteem for those previously labeled as "disengaged from the learning process" (Resta, 1998, p. 6).

Establishing Learning Communities

Mentoring relationships encourage collaboration, communication, and teamwork and provide ongoing support in both technology and pedagogy for both mentors and mentees. Such sharing resulted in the establishment of formal or informal learning communities. These learning communities emerged from a nurturing and supportive environment that allowed members to exchange ideas, share experiences, and learn together to accommodate individual learning styles (Stephen & Evans, 2000). In these mentoring models, learning communities existed within the group of mentors, between mentors and mentees, and in alliances of participating institutions with mentoring programs.

The structure of learning communities, created through mentoring, is not linear or hierarchical. Instead, these communities are asymmetric and connected by interaction and collaboration. In the models with mentoring as the field component of a course, learning communities resulted through communication (such as a listserv), e-mail, and face-to-face regular meetings (MacArthur et al., 1995; Sprague et al., 1998; Thompson et al., 1996). In this manner, mentors communicated with each other, shared experiences, and found solutions for technical and pedagogical problems. At New Mexico State University, one of the participating faculty members felt that "being a part of a faculty mentoring team usually developed a sense of belonging to the broader community of those committed to using educational technology" (Gonzales & Thompson, 1998, p. 169). At Mercyhurst College, their PT3 one-on-one mentoring program recruited graduate student mentors who were not technology savvy but were willing to learn and work together with faculty (Kennihan et al., 2004). One participant mentioned that, "working collaboratively is at the core of what makes this project so successful" (Kennihan et al., 2004, p. 3410). Historically, K–12 teachers tend to be isolated from their peers, so the development of a learning community of teachers through mentoring programs was particularly important. This was an emerging theme found in the extended mentoring models in K–12 environments (MacArthur et al., 1995).

Given the support of a learning community of both student mentors and faculty mentees, faculty members and teachers have the opportunity to learn, try, and to reinvent instructional technologies. Rogers (2003) described reinvention as "the degree to which an innovation is changed or modified by a user in the process of its adoption and implementation" (p. 180). The more reinvention occurs, the more rapidly an innovation is adopted and becomes institutionalized. The mentor models revealed that the one-on-one mentoring sessions help mentees become more confident about using instructional technologies and eventually, the mentees start to adapt technologies to meet their needs with help from the learning community. Thus, the faculty technology mentoring models provide faculty mentees with an active and collaborative learning environment that involves an adequate amount of trial ability of instructional technologies. One faculty member reflected on her mentoring experience:

> I began to see a whole new way of approaching my reading methods curriculum. After employing problem-based learning with technology, I found I could enter my methods class and find that students were already engaged in work. I was "hooked" into trying more creative and interactive practice. (Gonzales & Thompson, 1998, p. 167)

CONCLUSION

The literature suggests that one-on-one mentoring programs have successfully provided faculty in higher education and teachers in K–12 environments with expertise and support that they need in order to use and integrate technology. Mentoring programs were a part of many of the PT3 grant projects and PT3 grantees who initiated mentoring approaches as one way of faculty development confirm the effectiveness of the one-on-one approach.

Examination of the literature reveals that successful mentoring programs involve far more than merely assigning student mentors to faculty members or teachers. Characteristics of effective mentoring models include providing visions and setting goals, individualizing technology support, breaking down the hierarchical structure, establishing an open dialogue and collaborative relationships, and providing mutual benefits for mentors and mentees. In addition, successful programs resulted in the creation of learning communities of mentors and mentees. One of the strongest themes across the literature on successful programs was that a mentoring program needs to provide a community of support and communication for both mentors and mentees.

The stories from the field in the following chapters illustrate and expand upon the characteristics of successful mentoring programs as described in the literature. Knowledge gained from the literature and from the cases described in this book should provide both insights and specific strategies for educators who will be implementing technology staff development programs.

REFERENCES

Albion, P. R. (2001). Some factors in the development of self-efficacy beliefs for computer use among teacher education students. *TechTrends, 46*(5), 34–38.

Beisser, S. (2000). Technology mentorships in higher education: An optimal match for expanding educational computing skills. In B. Gillan & K. McFerrin (Eds.), *Faculty Development.* (ERIC Document Reproduction Service No ED444497).

Beisser, S., Kurth, J., & Reinhart, P. (1997). The teacher as learner: An undergraduate student and faculty mentorship success. In J. Willis, J. D. Price, S. McNeal, B. Robin & D. A. Willis (Eds.), *Technology and Teacher Education Annual, 1997,* (pp. 322–326). Charlottesville, VA: Association for the Advancement of Computing in Education.

Bramble, W. J. (2000). *U.S. Department of Education: Six month performance report. Project title: From shared vision to shared practice: Enabling tomorrow's teachers.* Albuquerque, NM: University of New Mexico, College of Education, Technology and Education Center.

Browne, N., Maeers, M., & Cooper, E. (2000). A faculty of education as a community of learners: Growing to meet the demands of instruction and technology. In B. Gillan & K. McFerrin (Eds.), *Faculty Development.* (ERIC Document Reproduction Service No ED444497).

Carlson, R. D/. & Gooden, J. S. (1999). Mentoring pre-service teachers for technology skills acquisition. In J. D. Price, J. Willis, D. A. Willis, M. Jost, & S. Boger-Mehall (Eds.), *Proceedings of SITE 99,* (pp. 1313–1318). Charlottesville, VA: Association for the Advancement of Computing in Education.

Cavanaugh, C. (2002). Faculty development in educational technology. In D. A. Willis, J. Price, & S. N. Davis (Eds.), *Information Technology and Teacher Education*

Annual, 2002, (pp. 621–622). Norfolk, VA: Association for the Advancement of Computing in Education.

Dougherty, W. V. (2000, January). Computer expertise: What expectations should we have of new teachers? *NASSP Bulletin, 84*(612), 72–77.

Dusick, D. M. (1998). What social cognitive factors influence faculty members' use of computers for teaching? Literature review. *Journal of Research on Computing in Education, 31*(2), 123–137.

Dwyer. J. (1998). *Work as professional development.* Queensland Consortium for Professional Development in Education. Annual Report, 1998. Retrieved September 3, 2001, from http://www.btr.qld.edu.au/Consortium/publ.html

Farenga, S. & Joyce, B. (1996, November). *Procedural knowledge teaching models: Effects of short-term Internet training of preservice teachers.* Paper presented at the 31st annual conference of the New York State Association for Computers and Technologies in Education. New York.

Franklin, T., Turner, S., Kariuki, M., & Duran, M. (2001). Mentoring overcomes barriers to technology integration. *Journal of Computing in Teacher Education, 18* (1), 26–31.

Generation www.Y. (2000). Generation www.Y annual reports: 4th annual performance report May, 2000. Retrieved November 8, 2001, from http://www.genyes.org/genwwwy/evaluations/annual4th.pdf

Generation www.Y. (2001). Generation www.Y: Teaching with technology. Retrieved November 8, 2001, from http://www.genyes.org/genwwwy

Gonzales, C., Hill, M., Leon, S., Orrantia, J., Saxton, M., & Sujo de Montes, L. (1997). Faculty from Mars, technology from Venus: Mentoring is the link. In J. Willis, J. D. Price, S. McNeal, B. Robin & D. A. Willis (Eds.), *Technology and Teacher Education Annual, 1997,* (pp. 327–330). Charlottesville, VA: Association for the Advancement of Computing in Education.

Gonzales, C. & Thompson, V. (1998). Reciprocal mentoring in technology use: Reflecting with a literacy educator. *Journal of Information Technology for Teacher Education,* 7(2), 163–176.

Hunt, J. M. (1961). *Intelligence and experience.* New York: Ronald Press.

Kennihan, T., Schaefer, M., & Hembrow Snyder, M. (2004). A PT3 project based collaborative learning model: Graduate assistants team model for professional development. In Crawford, C., Willis, D., Carlsen, R., Gibson, I., McFerrin, K., Price, J., & Weber, R. (Eds.), Proceedings *of Society for Information Technology and Teacher Education International Conference, 2004,* (pp. 3410–3411). Chesapeake, VA: Association for the Advancement of Computing in Education.

Javeri, M. & Hunt, E. (2002). Mentoring faculty to infuse technology throughout a pre-service teacher education program. In Crawford, C., Willis, D., Carlsen, R., Gibson, I., McFerrin, K., Price, J., Weber, R. (Eds.), *Proceedings of Society for Information Technology and Teacher Education International Conference, 2002,* (pp. 1640–1641). Chesapeake, VA: Association for the Advancement of Computing in Education.

Laffey, J. & Musser, D. (1998). Attitudes of preservice teachers about using technology in teaching. *Journal of Technology and Teacher Education, 6*(4), 223–242.

Leh, S. C. (2005). Lessons learned form service learning and reverse mentoring in faculty development: A case study in technology training. *Journal of Technology and Teacher Education, 13*(1), 25–41.

MacArthur, C. A., Pilato, V., Kercher, M., Peterson, D., Malouf, D., & Jamison, P. (1995). Mentoring: An approach to technology education for teachers. *Journal of Research on Computing in Education, 28*(1), 46–61.

Maushak, N., Kelley, P., & Blodgett, T. (2001). Preparing teachers for the inclusive classroom: A preliminary study of attitudes and knowledge of assistive technology. *Journal of Technology and Teacher Education, 9*(3), 419–431.

Milligan, K. & Robinson, S. (2000). Faculty development: From computer skills to technology integration. In B. Gillan & K. McFerrin (Eds.), *Faculty Development.* (ERIC Document Reproduction Service No ED444497).

O'Bannon, B., Mathew, K., & Thomas, L. (1998). Faculty development: Key to the integration of technology in teacher education, *Journal of Computing in Teacher Education, 14*(2), 7–11.

Office of Technology Assessment. (1995). *Teachers and technology: Making the connection.* (Report No. OTA-HER–616). Washington, DC: U.S. Government Printing Office.

Papert, S. (1980). *Mindstorms.* New York: Basic Books.

Philips-Jones, L. (1982). *Mentors and proteges.* New York: Arbor House.

Piller, B., Baek, E., & Leh, A. (2003). PT3 and training faculty to use technology—Reflections and perspectives. In Crawford, C., Willis, D., Carlsen, R., Gibson, I., McFerrin, K., Price, J., & Weber, R. (Eds.), Proceedings *of Society for Information Technology and Teacher Education International Conference, 2003,* (pp. 3645–3648). Chesapeake, VA: Association for the Advancement of Computing in Education.

PT3 (2004). *Faculty Development.* Retrieved October 23, 2004, from http://www.pt3.org/storiesstrategies/facultydevelopment/

Resta, P. (1998). *Collaborative technologies as a catalyst for changing teacher practices.* Washington, DC: Department of Education. (ERIC Document Reproduction Service No. ED428714).

Rivers, R. A., Eichelberger, A., & Ho, C. (2005). *Turning the tables: Students mentoring faculty to improve university teaching.* Retrieved September 3, 2005 from http://web.jmu.edu/iutconference/Eichelberger&Rivers.PDF

Rogers, E. M. (2003). *Diffusion of innovations* (5th edition). New York: Free Press.

Sandholtz, J. H. (2001). Learning to teach with technology: A comparison of teacher development programs. *Journal of Technology and Teacher Education, 9*(3), 349–374.

Schuttloffel, M. J. (2000). Teaching old dogs new tricks. In B. Gillan & K. McFerrin (Eds.), *Faculty Development.* (ERIC Document Reproduction Service No ED444497).

Smith, S. J. & O'Bannon, B. (1999). Faculty members infusing technology across teacher education: A mentorship model. *Teacher Education and Special Education, 22*(2), 123–135.

Sprague, D., Kopfman, K., & Dorsey, S. (1998). Faculty development in the integration of technology in teacher education courses. *Journal of Computing in Teacher Education, 14*(2), 24–28.

Stahlman, J., Nasara, A., & Abate, R. (2002). Faculty development with technology integration: A qualitative analysis of faculty mentoring. In Crawford, C., Willis, D., Carlsen, R., Gibson, I., McFerrin, K., Price, J., & Weber, R. (Eds.), *Proceedings of Society for Information Technology and Teacher Education International Conference 2002* (p. 600). Chesapeake, VA: Association for the Advancement of Computing in Education.

Stephen, M. L. & Evans, G. D. (2000, February). Edu-tech connect: A win-win endeavor. *Proceedings of Society for Information Technology & Teacher Education, San Diego, CA, 2000,* 2111–2114.

Stewart, E. B. (1999). Learning together: The use of mentoring for faculty development in the integration of technology. *Journal of Computing in Teacher Education, 16*(1), 15–19.

Strudler, N. & Wetzel, K. (1999). Lessons from exemplary colleges of education: Factors affecting technology integration in preservice programs. *Educational Technology Research and Development, 47*(4), 63–82.

Strudler, N., Archambault, L., Bendixen, L., Anderson, D., & Weiss, R. (2003). Project THREAD: Technology helping restructure educational access and delivery. *Educational Technology Research and Development, 51*(1), 41–56.

Stuhlman, J. (1998). A model for infusing technology into teacher training programs. *Journal of Technology and Teacher Education, 6*(2/3), 1125–1140.

Thompson, A., Hansen D., & Reinhart, P. (1996). One-on-one technology mentoring for teacher education faculty: Case study reports. In B. Robin, J. D. Price, J. Willis, & D. A. Willis (Eds.), *Technology and Teacher Education Annual, 1996,* (pp. 495–498). Charlottesville, VA: Association for the Advancement of Computing in Education.

Thompson, A., Schmidt, D., & Davis, N. (2003). Technology collaboratives for simultaneous renewal in teacher education. *Educational Technology Research and Development, 51*(1), 73–89.

Tyler-Wood, T., Christensen, R., Arrowood, D., Allen, J., & Maldonado, M. (2000). *Implementing technology into preservice teacher courses: PT3 first year accomplishments.* Retrieved October 8, 2001, from http://pt3.org/project_desc.php3?grantee_id=121

Zachariades, I. G., & Roberts, S. K. (1995). A collaborative approach to helping teacher education faculty model integration in their courses: An informal case. *Journal of Technology and Teacher Education, 3*(4), 351–357.

Zachary, L. (2001). *Mentoring at a distance: Strategies for success.* U.S. Department of Education Star Schools Project, Distance Learning Resource Network Web Site. Retrieved November 15, 2001, from http://www.dlrn.org/library/dl/mentoring.html.

CHAPTER 4

A SENIOR FACULTY MEMBER APPROACHES TECHNOLOGY

Denise Lindstrom and Geoff Abelson

A FACULTY MEMBER DECIDES TO CHANGE

> The process of change for the teaching profession between 1990 and 2020 will be painful for most of the existing teaching force, however enterprise will be rewarded and leaders will emerge at all levels among teachers. (Hargraves, 1997)

This case study describes the change process for a successful senior faculty member in the Department of Curriculum and Instruction at Iowa State University. Specifically, this faculty member, through his involvement in the technology mentoring program, learned how to create PowerPoint slide shows to replace overhead transparencies in his lectures and then went on to explore additional ways technology could assist student learning. Convincing senior faculty members to use newer technologies in their teaching practices can be especially difficult. It is not required of them and it is extremely time consuming to become proficient in using new technologies. Faculty members who take the initiative to go through the process of change need to be commended. The choice to incorporate technology into their teaching demonstrates their commitment to life long learning both to their peers, and to their students. This kind of modeling by faculty

Faculty Mentoring: The Power of Students in Developing Technology Expertise, pages 47–57

members, like Dr. Geoff Abelson, needs to occur for the successful and widespread integration of technology into education.

FACULTY PROFILE

Dr. Abelson has been a member of the Iowa State University Department of Curriculum and Instruction since 1977. He received his doctorate at the University of Michigan after spending seven years as a special education teacher in both the elementary and secondary grades. He began to use computers first as "decoration for his office" but then, like me, learned to use them for word processing and e-mail.

Dr. Abelson, like most teachers, learned to use his computer independently. He had made it a goal to learn one new thing every day until he could use his computer to write and print documents. It took him three weeks to accomplish this. Dr. Abelson had attended two computer workshops provided by the technical support community at the university. He didn't find them helpful because he felt they were geared toward people who had more experience with computers than he did. The trainings were according to Dr. Abelson, either over his head or didn't have anything to do with what he needed to know. Dr. Abelson decided that he wanted to learn PowerPoint because he had seen other colleagues using it and he felt it presented information more clearly and effectively. He also felt that it was "what students expected these days."

MENTOR PROFILE

I entered the mentoring program at Iowa State University as a first semester graduate student in Curriculum and Instructional Technology. Prior to that, I had taught sixth grade for 3 years in Oakland, California and in the process had become intrigued with the use of computers in the classroom. My use of computers had been limited to basic word processing and some Internet searching but I had seen some of my colleagues begin to use computers for multimedia and Internet related activities with their students. Teachers using computers in this way were still very much in the minority, but it was easy to recognize the positive and engaging impact this kind of teaching was having on students.

When I had an opportunity to attend graduate school, I knew immediately that I wanted to focus on Instructional Technology. Although my computer skills were limited, I had just added e-mail to my repertoire of skills, I was offered a teaching assistantship in an undergraduate course designed to teach prospective teachers how to effectively integrate technology into their future classrooms. Thus, I was required to learn software programs, like Excel and HyperStudio, and how to use hardware, like scanners and digital cameras, so that I could help my students complete their class projects. This assistantship also required me to work at the service desk in the Center for Technology in Learning and Teaching (CTLT). As a result of being forced to troubleshoot technology problems for several hours a day, my technology skills immediately began to increase. However, I perceived myself to be very much a novice user, especially when compared with the other teaching and students assistants I worked with in the CTLT. Therefore, I was hesitant when my advisor suggested that I might benefit by enrolling in the Technology in Teacher Education Mentoring Program. I was convinced I had little to offer anyone, especially a faculty member, in the way of aiding in the development of their technology skills.

After the first class meeting I began to feel better about my abilities to serve as a mentor. The instructor stressed that we were not expected to act as experts but that the mentor-mentee relationship would be one of shared growth. It has been observed, "Prima Donnas and stars rarely make good mentors. They can be intimidating and off-putting. Knowledge and skill are less important than empathy and nurturing qualities" (McKenzie, 1998). I had empathy; especially for anyone who felt that one wrong move with a computer might result in all your hard work being instantaneously wiped out.

The professor of the course took the skill level of the mentors and mentees into consideration. The mentoring program was designed to pay attention to the compatibility of instructional technology with faculty specific needs. In Chapter 2, Sahin described that when instructional technologies are compatible with the faculty needs, the rate of the adoption of these technologies will increase based on Rogers' (2003) theory. As the professor of the class had recruited the faculty members she developed an idea of the computer skills or programs each person wanted to learn. The faculty members were then paired with mentors who either had at least some technology knowledge in the area of interest or were at least interested in gaining the same skill as the faculty member. So it seemed natural that I should be paired with Geoff who had expressed a desire to learn PowerPoint. I had created and given my first PowerPoint presentation just a week earlier and was eager to become more proficient with the program. The following sections describe how we overcame the complex issue of adopting the PowerPoint software application into Dr. Abelson's teaching and how he would finally be able to create a PowerPoint presentation by himself.

THE POWERPOINT SESSIONS

Dr. Abelson and I began our mentor–mentee relationship with much in common. We had about the same level of experience with computers and

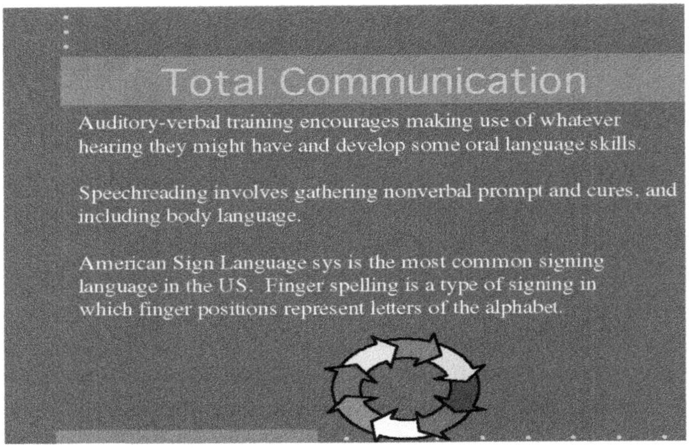

Figure 4.1. Dr. Abelson's first PowerPoint slide.

we both had a strong desire to become more technologically savvy in order to improve our teaching. I was still nervous about my lack of expertise with PowerPoint, but Dr. Abelson proved to be understanding and patient with the process. It was clear he understood the nature of the relationship.

We were learning together and he did not expect me to know all of the answers or to hold his hand. We spent an average of one to two hours a week working together on PowerPoint (see Figure 4.1). I think Dr. Abelson found the experience most beneficial because I provided him with a regular, *set aside,* period of time that was dedicated to learning the new technology. It was also beneficial tome because I took it upon myself to find the answers to problems that we could not figure out together during our sessions. I did this by either reading the program manual, or, more often, tracking down a person who was more knowledgeable. At our first meeting we set the goal to create a presentation for one of his lectures and to present it. In the beginning I felt that this goal would be accomplished in a month or so, but I was wrong. This experience has impressed upon me the incredible amount of time and energy it takes to make a switch to a newer form of technology. Learning the software was only a piece of the challenge, as we had to deal with numerous unexpected hardware issues and basic classroom organizational dilemmas. However, with support from the staff in the CTLT and the Department of Curriculum and Instruction we were provided with an environment in which we could experiment and through our failures eventually succeed. Which, according to Rogers (2003), is an important step in the adoption of an innovation.

One of the hardware challenges involved the use of a laptop. In order to give a PowerPoint presentation in the lecture hall we needed to take a laptop with us. That led to the need for a zip drive to download the presentation that had been created on Dr. Abelson's desktop computer, so that it could be uploaded to the laptop. We soon discovered the need for special software that allowed the zip drive to function on Dr. Abelson's desktop computer. This discovery was made during a session in which we crashed his computer at least five times while trying to use the zip drive without the appropriate software. Frustrated and frantic, we sought help from the student assistants in the CTLT and from the technical support people in the Department of Curriculum and Instruction. They all added solutions to the problem and patiently showed us where to get, and how to load, the specific software needed. Through all this Dr. Abelson maintained the mindset that this was a learning experience for both of us, which helped alleviate my nervousness about my own technological shortcomings. This experience was also connecting him to resources, like the students assistants at the CTLT service desk that he could use for other technical difficulties in the future, ultimately making him a more independent technology user.

Geoff had been using an overhead projector for years to deliver his lectures and had a manila folder full of overhead transparencies. Part of his normal preparation for lectures entailed shuffling through this folder of overheads to find the specific overheads needed for that day's lecture. While our initial goal was to create one slideshow for one lecture, it soon became reorganizing and transforming all of his overhead transparencies into digital slides and then creating individual slideshows for the lectures. This task led to our first organizational issue and once again proved to be more difficult than I had originally predicted. Dr. Abelson was not comfortable with predetermining how much material would be covered in a lecture. His style dictated that the amount of material covered was determined by student questions and interactions. Therefore, instead of organizing the slides into shows for each individual lecture, we decided to organize them by topic, which gave Dr. Abelson the freedom he needed for his lectures.

After we made that decision, another frustration surfaced. We realized that this task was not a matter of simple direct transfer of information from transparency to slide. By its very nature, a PowerPoint slide requires different size chunks of information than an overhead, and if we were going to go through all of the effort of transferring the information, we felt it was important to take PowerPoint to its full potential and add graphics and animation. This capability is one of the important features that make PowerPoint a more effective medium for the delivery of information. It has the ability to address visual and audio learning styles to capture the attention of today's digital age students.

After we had nailed down the basics of choosing a background, templates, adding slides, editing slides, viewing slides, finding slide templates, and exploring the graphics library and preset animation, we were ready to make slides (Figure 4.2). With all the options to consider the process was slowed down considerably. We produced an average of three slides a ses-

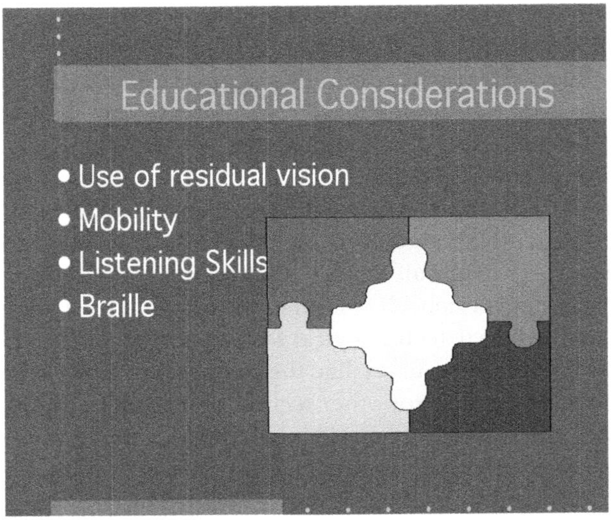

Figure 4.2. Improving the PowerPoint slide making process.

sion. While the process was enjoyable, Dr. Abelson had nearly one hundred overhead transparencies and thus, the process was lengthy. I began to worry that he might be discouraged by the amount of time it was taking to create slides. However, he appeared to remain engaged and enthusiastic about becoming more familiar with the technology as we progressed. We continued making slides for the rest of the semester.

MAKING A DECISION TO CONTINUE THE MENTORING PROCESS

As the semester came to a close Dr. Abelson and I mastered the intricacies involved in making PowerPoint slides, organizing PowerPoint slides, and printing PowerPoint slides. However, we did not meet the original goal of actually giving a lecture with PowerPoint slides. We had come such a long way and we were so close to meeting our goal that I hoped Dr. Abelson would want me to continue mentoring him the following semester. I knew exactly what Dr. Abelson needed to do in order to have his lectures complete with PowerPoint presentations.

REACHING THE POWERPOINT GOAL

During the winter break Dr. Abelson had continued to make slides on his own and by the start of the spring semester was ready to conduct his first lecture with PowerPoint. I began to accompany him to his lectures to help set up the laptop, hook up the projector, and help with other technical difficulties involved with making PowerPoint presentations in a lecture hall.

In anticipation of his starting the new semester with PowerPoint supported lectures, I had ordered a remote mouse for Dr. Abelson's use. Dr. Abelson had been concerned about getting trapped behind the computer in order to advance the PowerPoint slides as needed. The remote gave him the freedom necessary to interact with his students and still run the presentation.

In the beginning I took responsibility for transferring the slideshows from the desktop computer to the laptop computer, setting up the laptop in the lecture hall, and making sure the projector was running properly. After Dr. Abelson became comfortable with running the PowerPoint slideshow, I gradually showed him how to do all those things.

For a while I arranged for a fellow T.A. to go with Dr. Abelson to his lectures, if for some reason I couldn't make it. Even though I felt he was capable of performing the whole task on his own, he expressed a considerable amount of anxiety at the thought of it. After about eight weeks, there came a time where it wasn't possible for me or someone else to accompany him to lecture. He was going to have to do it alone. The day before we went through the process to make sure he was ready. I didn't want him to experience failure or become so frustrated with the technology that he would choose to give it up.

As it turned out, Dr. Abelson successfully accomplished the entire process on his own. In fact, he ended up receiving a round of spontaneous applause from his students after he set up the laptop and turned on the projector unassisted. Apparently the students had been aware of his struggles and they were impressed and appreciative of his efforts. This incident also speaks to the mentoring program's power to provide environments for the "observability" factor in the adoption of innovation. The visibility of Dr. Abelson's struggle and success in using technology, according to Rogers (2003), may aid in the adoption of technology infusion into teaching by his preservice teachers.

DR. ABELSON'S PERSPECTIVE

I am a professor of special education and have been a faculty member for more than 20 years. The opportunity of having a graduate student in instructional technology mentor me in the use of PowerPoint was immediately appealing. I teach an introductory course each semester with an enrollment of about 200. I have always relied on overhead slides for supplementing my lectures. For several years, I have been interested in developing the skills to use PowerPoint to improve the quality and aesthetic appeal of my classroom presentations.

I have been accessing the Internet and e-mail on a regular basis since about 1993. My learning experiences were slow, tedious and frustrating. I learned that I am a fairly concrete learner of technology, and I need the "hands on" kind of assistance. I did not benefit from two short on-campus courses designed to help novices. Rather, I learned to use e-mail and the Internet by learning one skill a day from a colleague. Within, three weeks, I developed some very limited, functional computer skills. Having a mentor provide instruction in my office, on my own computer, is exactly what I needed to sharpen my technology skills and to learn PowerPoint. Further, the thought of having a mentor to call on for problem solving has increased my comfort level in learning to use PowerPoint.

My mentor and I usually meet on a prearranged twice-weekly basis in my office. Each session lasts about an hour. This has been happening for more than six months. My initial goal of receiving mentoring was to become adept at preparing and presenting PowerPoint slides. I am on the way to my goal, but I am still very dependent on my mentor for problem solving and learning new techniques to implement PowerPoint.

My experiences in learning PowerPoint have been very positive and reinforcing. There have been periods of frustration, but these are short term and usually resolved after consultation from my mentor. I view the mentoring relationship as a learning experience for both of us, and do not expect "magical" progress.

The first few mentoring sessions involved familiarizing me with the virtues and attributes of PowerPoint and some of the logistical basics necessary to setup PowerPoint slides. My mentor prepared "how to" listings of PowerPoint basics including creating a new slide show and adding clip art and preset animation. The listings are similar to recipes with specific steps. I have the steps taped on a bookshelf adjacent to my computer. These step-by-step listings, however, have not replaced my need for "hands on" assistance.

Over the ensuing months, I have converted old overhead slides to new PowerPoint slides and have created new slides from new material for the course. For a number of weeks, I required the presence of my mentor to prepare either type of PowerPoint slide. This meant that my mentor spent many hours sitting beside my desk, watching me prepare new slides, and occasionally answering a question or redirecting me in order to problem solve. At the time, I perceived this experience to be arduous and boring for my mentor. Then slowly, I began to attain the skills necessary to prepare PowerPoint slides independently. A full fall semester, 16 weeks, was required for me to develop the "entry level" skills necessary to begin to make PowerPoint presentations, on a regular basis in spring semester.

For nearly four weeks, my mentor accompanied me to class on Mondays, Wednesdays, and Fridays, in addition to the usual mentoring in my office for two hours per week. My most frustrating moments occurred when my mentor and I had difficulty with PowerPoint in the presence of 200 students. This happened in two class sessions as I recall. After that initial "bumpy" start, the two of us successfully provided PowerPoint Presentations to class.

Then one afternoon my mentor informed me that she had a previous commitment and that I would be doing the PowerPoint presentation alone at the next class meeting. This prospect raised considerable anxieties, but nothing bad happened. Whew! In fact, the class applauded when I appeared without the mentor and successfully showed the first PowerPoint slide. This was a time of celebration for me and I immediately told my mentor. Clearly, the two of us deserved the applause. After this solo experience, my mentor began providing on site assistance on a rather intermittent basis strengthening my independence. There is a campus phone in the lecture hall, and I have occasionally used it in desperation to call my mentor, i.e., when I had difficulty turning on the support mechanism for the screen.

CONCLUSION

After reading Dr. Abelson's perspective on the mentoring experience he had with me, I am convinced of the theory that "there's great emotional support that comes from a live body who uses clear and nontechnical language and who has the social skills to make teachers feel good about their forays into this new strange land" (Technology Briefs, 1995). The phrase, "this new strange land" is intended to mean "technology integration into education." In a study conducted by Smith and O'Bannon (1999), the working assumption is made that graduate students regardless of their technology expertise can offer support. Their study involved using graduate students with little experience using PowerPoint to become mentors for faculty members learning PowerPoint. The results of their study mirror my lived experience. They found that technical expertise is not a prerequisite for being a successful mentor. They also found that the lack of technical expertise appeared to work in the favor of the student mentors. Faculty in their study reported that, "the environment that the special education mentors created was nonthreatening. Instead of being considered the technology expert, many members commented on how they explored the complexities of the software together. They appreciated that the students were learning themselves and felt that they understood their inexperience with the PowerPoint application."(Smith & O'Bannon, 1999, p. 130).

Dr. Abelson saw that technology offers many advantages for improving teaching, is easy to learn, and is compatible with his teaching strategies and needs (respectively, referring to relative advantage, simplicity, and compatibility attributes of innovations). Dr. Abelson expressed interest in integrating technology into his teaching even further by developing a web page for his course and possibly using an on-line classroom for some activities for his students. I think that Dr. Abelson's continued interest in learning technology is due to the positive learning environment that mentoring can create. Not only does it humanize technology, it provides the situational learning experiences that create the greatest amount of relevancy for learners. As the mentor, it was often unsettling and stressful to have no idea what the day's meeting with Dr. Abelson might bring. There was little I could do to prepare for our time together. Our agenda was created as new challenges arose in order to meet our technology goal.

NEXT STEP

Dr. Abelson and I still continue our mentor–mentee relationship even though he has been paired with a new mentor for the fall semester. He was given the use of a new laptop computer to use for his lectures and he needed some help learning to use it. I gave him a refresher session on loading the PowerPoint presentations onto the new computer. Dr. Abelson followed up on his interest in using the on-line classroom Blackboard.com. He is using it to communicate with his students using the e-mail features and to post his course procedures, expectations and class schedule electronically instead of using handouts. I helped him learn how to use these features and continue to support him when he runs into trouble using Blackboard.com. He is comfortable in letting me know when he needs help and I look forward to seeing him and being involved with his continued progress in using new technologies in his teaching. I believe the change in Dr. Abelson's technology use will positively affect non or low users of technology in the college. Our case is another success story of the mentoring program showing its role in diffusing instructional technologies in teacher education programs and facilitating faculty change in the uses of these technologies.

REFERENCES

Hargraves, D. (1997). A road to the learning society. *School Leadership and Management*, 17(1), 20.

McKenzie, J. (1998). Creating learning cultures with just-in-time support. *Staff Professional Development & Adult Learning for School Education Teachers.* Retrieved August 28, 2005, from http://staffdevelop.org/adult.html .

Rogers, E. M. (2003). *Diffusion of innovations* (5th ed.). New York, NY: Free Press.

Smith, J., & O'Bannon B., (1999). Faculty members infusing technology across teacher education: A mentorship model. *Teacher Education and Special Education, 22*(2), 123–135.

Technology Briefs. (1995). *Technology: The training of staff.* Retrieved August 25, 2000, from http://www.nea.org/cet/briefs/11.html.

CHAPTER 5

MAKING CONNECTIONS

An International Student's Perspective

Hsueh-Hua Chuang

Mentoring is typically defined as the sharing of knowledge and skills through a mentor's support, guidance, and feedback to a mentee. In addition to these characteristics, the faculty technology mentoring program at Iowa State University provides the opportunity for both mentors and mentees to enhance cultural awareness, to break down traditional hierarchical barriers, and to experience learner-centered learning through continuous reciprocal mentoring relationships. Bandura's Social Learning Theory emphasizes the importance of observing and modeling behaviors and emotional reactions of others, and indicates that human behaviors are the results of continuous interactions among cognitive, behavioral, and environmental influences (Bandura, 1977). This case study focuses upon the human relationship part of the mentoring program with an emphasis on the mutual benefits for mentor and mentee.

As the student mentor in this case, I was able to build self-efficacy as a technology mentor, since I felt valued and supported. The two faculty mentees increased their familiarity with computer-related technologies and began to envision the integration of these technologies into their teaching. As an international graduate student mentor, I needed to overcome my culturally ingrained anxiety about not being a perfectly knowledgeable, experienced technology mentor. I increased my confidence as a technology

Faculty Mentoring: The Power of Students in Developing Technology Expertise, pages 59–69

Figure 5.1. Working with one faculty mentee in her office.

mentor by seeing myself possessing the capabilities needed to perform a task, via verbal persuasion from my mentees. I worked with two faculty members, and gained insightful pedagogical expertise in an authentic educational environment that emphasized collaboration, communication, and teamwork. I appreciated the opportunity to be involved with the mentoring program. It provided me not only a chance to work and build connections with faculty in a one-on-one situation, but also gave me the opportunity to experience true collaboration (see Figure 5.1). This mentoring experience is indeed one of the highlights of my graduate student career.

FACULTY PROFILES

Professor Carol Fuhler

Professor Fuhler is an associate professor of Literacy Education and also the Assistant Chair in the Department of Curriculum and Instruction. Both students and faculty respect her as an outstanding teacher in the department. She teaches graduate children's literature courses and undergraduate reading methods courses. Prior to the mentoring experience, Professor Fuhler's technology experience involved mainly the use of e-mail and word processing. She also knew how to search Amazon.com for the most up-to-date book reviews and related information. As a result of participating in the faculty technology mentoring program as a mentee, she expected to increase her familiarity with class management software tools, to make good use of the personal computer in her office, and to learn to integrate technology into her teaching activities.

Professor Fuhler mentioned that she had limited experience with the computer and did not learn easily from direction sheets, so the mentoring process of learning at her own pace and receiving on-site, individualized technology assistance was very appealing to her. Despite her limited experience with computer-related technology, she felt a strong need to integrate computer technology into her personal life, teaching, and her administrative career.

Instructor Denise Zumbach

Ms. Zumbach is a temporary instructor in the Department of Curriculum and Instruction. She teaches undergraduate reading methods and science methods courses. Ms. Zumbach already had a powerful Macintosh laptop and was determined to learn the "ins and outs" of this computer. In fact, she was not new to the faculty technology mentoring program. Her previous mentoring experience gave her a start, and she wanted to move forward with more technology assistance. Most of her computer knowledge resulted from trial and error. The computer in her office had limited memory, so it froze on her several times a day when she switched between programs. She felt frustrated and thought the computer needed to be upgraded. Ms. Zumbach used the computer for e-mail, word processing, and Internet searching. She hoped to learn some advanced e-mail procedures, such as adding a signature and organizing address books. She was also interested in creating digital images to improve her desktop publishing documents and in using PowerPoint to replace her overhead transparencies. She felt that a good command of computer knowledge would help her teach more effectively.

STUDENT MENTOR PROFILE

Hsueh-Hua Chuang

I entered the faculty technology mentoring program by taking the course entitled Technology in Teacher Education (CI 610) as a first-semester doctoral student in the Department of Curriculum and Instruction. I earned my master's degree in Curriculum and Instructional Technology with a specialization in computer-based instruction applied to second/foreign language teaching in 1994 from the State University of New York at Albany. Prior to entering the Iowa State University doctoral program, I was an EFL (English as a Foreign Language) teacher in a high school in Taiwan. My technology experiences were mostly on the Windows platform, ranging from desktop publishing to using web page software packages. I would not describe myself as an advanced technology user, but my previous degree did allow me to explore some possibilities in terms of computer-based learning. However, being a technology mentor to a faculty member was something I had never considered. It was with great anxiety that I started my first mentoring journey.

The Mentoring Experience (I)

I was paired with Professor Fuhler and Ms. Zumbach with whom I shared similar academic backgrounds in the fields of language and reading. However, I was worried about trouble-shooting in front of them when I thought I was supposed to be a knowledgeable technology mentor. Despite my doubts, I considered the mentoring program a good opportunity to reduce the sense of isolation commonly felt by many international students in American colleges and to make connections with faculty. We first corresponded by e-mail and decided to meet once every two weeks for two hours instead of one hour every week so that we would have more time to explore the technology between sessions.

The First Meeting. Professor Fuhler politely greeted me the first time we met in her office. We then started with the software programs that were on her computer. She indicated that she had problems the last time she used a spreadsheet. I helped her by building a grading sheet for her class and guided her step-by-step so that she would know the structure of Excel. I demonstrated the format functions for cells, rows, and columns. I helped her remember them by showing her the icons on the tool bar above the worksheet. Professor Fuhler was very surprised that it was so easy to understand. Previously, she thought it was something so complicated that she was afraid to explore it. She preferred to do her grading manually with pencil, paper, and a calculator; however, she made mistakes every semester no matter how careful she was. There were always students coming to her for grade corrections. When I showed her the functions and formulas in Excel, which can automatically calculate the grades and the percentages, she was pleased and could not stop admiring the wonderful software program. With some guidance from me, she built her first grade sheet using Excel. This was the first triumph of my mentoring journey and I felt very encouraged and looked forward to our next meeting. As mentioned by Sahin in Chapter 2, providing observability and simplicity can decrease the level of anxiety and uncertainty for the faculty mentees and thus will result in successful adoption of innovations. This small triumph provided both the observability and simplicity attributes for the mentee and helped move us forward in the adoption process.

Moving Ahead with Software Programs. Our relationship continued to build as we learned to trouble shoot together. There were times when I, too, suddenly forgot where to locate the icons or the function keys to make the spreadsheet work. I would resort to trial and error tactics until I figured it out. At first I felt a little embarrassed, but Professor Fuhler was understanding and agreed that people learn by making mistakes! When I was doing my trouble-shooting, she would show me the application direction sheets and manuals she had, hoping that they would be helpful to me. By working with me in the trouble-shooting process, she also learned to solve some computer problems on her own. As we became comfortable trouble-shooting together, our personal, collaborative relationship grew.

At first I had to help her get started, but she eventually began taking the initiative to create things on her own. When she created an Excel grade sheet on her own, I was just there for assistance. I felt a sense of achievement and I could see that she was moving toward the reinvention stage of adoption, which increased my confidence level as a technology mentor. My initial anxiety, about not knowing it all myself, gradually dissolved.

For the next few months, we worked with different applications. We also talked about how to integrate technology into teaching activities. Professor Fuhler wanted to update her childrens book reviews using PowerPoint presentations, so she wouldn't have to carry several heavy books to pass around to the students each time the class met. I told her that we could even use PowerPoint to make external links to related resources, so the presentation would be more dynamic. She gladly accepted the idea. Then we started making her first slide show, starting with a digital image of her, which I took using a digital camera. I helped her insert images from disks or directly from the Internet into the slide show. Then we added background colors, edited the text, and inserted the graphic design. Professor Fuhler never failed to give me an emotional boost when I showed her how to complete an aspect of a slide show project. I also felt that I was gaining more confidence about my technology knowledge. Being a mentor helped me understand the details of several software applications, and, as it turned out, I benefited even more than my mentee.

Web Page. Professor Fuhler also mentioned that she wanted to build her own web page. We discussed the idea of a preproduction period before actually building a web site. We brainstormed what the web page's main purpose would be. We also discussed the target audience, the design of pages, and the connection to learning and teaching. After we clarified some ideas, we started with Claris Homepage. I guided her through some web page basics such as page title, text editing, backgrounds, tables, anchors, local and external links, and consolidating. Again, we didn't do it all in a rush. I allowed her some time to try by herself. Later, she was actually working on a homepage of her own. In one of her e-mail messages to me, she proudly told me that she was doing her homework. I told Professor Fuhler that she could always contact me for further assistance even when the semester's mentoring work was over. I cherished her trust in me and I enjoyed working with her collaboratively.

The Mentoring Experience (II)

My mentoring experience with Ms. Denise Zumbach was quite another story even though we used primarily the same application as I had with Professor Fuhler. Ms. Zumbach organized our schedule and set up meeting times for the whole semester the first time we met. She also assigned a learning unit to each of the meeting times. This served as a checklist when we were exploring a certain software application. Ms. Zumbach viewed the computer as an excellent tool to support her work in preparing for class. She wanted to learn how to generate PowerPoint slides for class lectures, design lesson plans, use Excel for grading, and learn some desktop publishing skills.

The Hardware Challenge. I checked out a digital camera from the Center for Technology in Learning and Teaching the first time we met and then showed Ms. Zumbach the different graphic formats. I then inserted images into her PowerPoint slides. At that time, we were still using her old desktop computer with very little memory, and she had to constantly close one program in order to switch to another one. She was getting very impatient with the old machine. We encountered several other technical problems. The inserted image didn't show up on the PowerPoint slide so I began troubleshooting. I installed an image-converting program, and it worked. However, she was still frustrated by the old computer, especially when she switched between programs, and a dialogue box popped out warning her that there was not enough memory.

Then we tried a scanner. Ms. Zumbach was busy clicking on the icons. Before I showed her some basics of Color It, a graphic software program allowing users to rescale, flip the scanned image, and save the image in some appropriate format, Ms. Zumbach would rotate the picture on the scanner and rescan it rather than use the software to rotate it. It was interesting. I began to settle into a mentoring pattern with Ms. Zumbach, letting her go explore the technology on her own, for she is a visual learner and a risk taker as well.

Working on a Laptop. Later, we were able to work on Ms. Zumbach's laptop, which did allow us more freedom to go between programs, so that we could deal with graphic images more efficiently. Together we went through desktop publishing, making newsletters, and adding graphic design elements to a word document. I also convinced her to use Excel as a grade book. She was reluctant in the beginning, because she didn't have very many students, so it wouldn't take her long to record and calculate the grades manually. However, after I showed her how to enter and manipulate data in a spreadsheet using Excel, she realized that it was a good tool and, most of all, not very complicated. She couldn't wait to create a spreadsheet for each of her classes. Basically, for Ms. Zumbach, I was more like a tech support and solution center. My role ranged from helping her add a signature to outgoing e-mail messages in Eudora, an e-mail program, to finding appropriate software applications for particular purposes in her teaching. There were times when I couldn't come up with immediate solutions for her software needs or problems, but together we would call someone for assistance or I would later e-mail or call her with a solution. She felt more and more comfortable working with her laptop computer.

Personal Relationship. My relationship with Ms. Zumbach was similar to friends who share some common interests and try to help each other. Besides working on the computer needs or problems, we shared with each other our family lives and our hobbies, and exchanged opinions on certain issues. We talked about how to raise kids in a bilingual environment. She told me how she wished she could speak fluent German like her parents do. She once showed me a Chinese Cinderella fairy tale in English and asked me if I was familiar with the story. I read the story for the first time and found that the original Chinese tale was written thousands of years ago in classic Chinese. It was actually quite different from contemporary Chinese language. Ms. Zumbach wanted to know if the English translation accurately presented the original tale in Chinese. Although I received some training in high school to read Classic Chinese, I experienced some difficulties in understanding several paragraphs in the Chinese Cinderella fairy tale. I called a friend in Taiwan for some help to fully comprehend the story. It was a good learning experience for me. We actually enjoyed a good discussion on the fairy tales of "East meets West." We even shared this experience with all the participants in the mentoring program in our annual mentor-mentee luncheon (see Figure 5.2).

REDEFINE THE WORD "MENTOR"

I am from a culture which views mentors/teachers/instructors as omnipotent authority figures. This background interfered with my initial ability to see how the mentoring experience could be expanded into my own culture. As Denise Lindstrom described in Chapter 4, the mentor-mentee experience is one of shared growth. As I grew more comfortable in learn-

Figure 5.2. Talking and sharing in annual mentor-mentee luncheon.

ing with my mentee, I was relieved and more willing to try new tasks, ideas, and technologies without fearing that I might expose my weak points. This was not allowed in my initial concept of mentoring. However, with the vision encouraged in the one-on-one mentoring program, I developed a new, positive attitude towards technology and increased the level of confidence in my own technology skills. For me, the relationship built in the faculty technology mentoring program is a reciprocal one. The word mentor can be synonymous with tutor, facilitator, buddy expert, consultant, collaborator, supporter, helper, and even good listener. The mutual benefits really made my mentoring experiences dynamic and rewarding.

Before this mentoring experience, I did not think that the student mentor-teacher approach would be feasible for me given the cultural background with which I grew up. I could not imagine how students would be able to mentor teachers. When, in fact, a successful technology mentoring program involves more than simply assigning graduate students to teach the faculty about technology, I realize that the establishment of learning communities is the key to the "student teach teacher" approach regardless of diverse cultural backgrounds. The technology mentoring program is about learning from each other instead of teaching others. Bandura (1977) proposed that observational learning or modeling is a central theme in Social Learning Theory and observational learning is most likely to occur when the model behavior is rewarded, and the observer is more likely to reproduce the rewarded behavior. Therefore, celebrating and sharing the accomplishments of each member in the learning community formed through the mentoring program contributes to the success of this student teaching teacher (STT) approach. I now see the feasibility of adopting a similar STT approach as faculty development in my own culture because of its focus on intergenerational observational learning. Although it will be somewhat challenging to establish such a program in my country, I believe that I now have the knowledge, confidence and skill to pursue this goal.

A LEARNING COMMUNITY

Carroll (2000) distinguished a learning community from a community of learners and he emphasized that in a community of learners each individual is engaged in his or her own learning. Therefore, the emergence of a learning community lays the foundation of a community of learners who can work collaboratively. Each member of the collaboration is in the position of learning within the community, drawing on the expertise of other group members (Sergiovanni, 1994). In classrooms as learning communities, according to the educational philosophy of a community of learners with a sociocultural approach emphasizing learning and development (Vygotsky, 1978), the students and the teachers collaboratively share responsibility and ownership for guidance and learning (Dewey, 1966; Rogoff, Matusov, & White, 1996). This case study showcases a good example of intergenerational collaborative learning shared by both graduate students and faculty members. In Chapter 2, Sahin described this collaboration as an interpersonal communication channel based on Rogers' (2003) theory; this interpersonal communication is very influential in the innovation decision process to adopt an innovation.

Professor Fuhler concluded that it would be impossible for her to learn all of the software programs by using the manuals, and she felt that with a mentor, she could grasp the core of technology. Most of all, she felt supported and challenged to learn more. After watching me do trouble-shooting, she even tried to work things out on her own. I saw this aspect as the most valuable part in the mentor/mentee experience. Ms. Zumbach was also willing to take more risks in trying different software programs. From my perspective, I see these attitudes as positive reinforcement for using technology in teaching.

Mentoring forced me to advance my own computer knowledge, because I could never anticipate what would happen or what computer problems I would encounter the next time I was to meet my mentees. Thanks to the faculty and staff in the Center for Technology in Teaching and Learning (CTLT), and the "people helping people" atmosphere there, I felt strongly

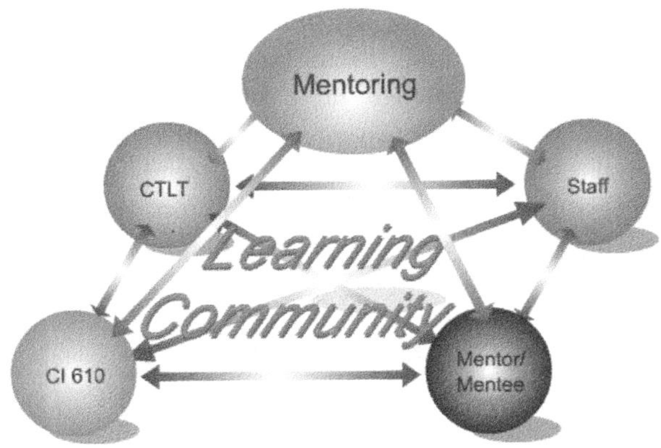

Figure 5.3. The learning community model at Iowa State University.

supported as a first-time mentor. Through this experience, I learned the solutions to all kinds of hardware and software problems.

In addition, we were allowed to share our latest mentoring experiences in the course that accompanied the experience. With the instructor's guiding assistance in our weekly face-to-face meeting and by working with other peer mentors as a team, I gradually gained the skills needed to mentor a faculty member. Furthermore, I overcame my anxiety of not being able to provide an immediate answer to my mentees. I originally thought that a mentor was a person who was omnipotent. When I reflected on the mentoring experience of the past semester, I was strongly aware of the fact that I learned not only by mentoring but by tackling obstacles with the support of a learning community, including the efforts of people from the class itself, my peer mentors, and the CTLT (see Figure 5.3). Being a mentor did not mean that I mastered all of the technology skills, but it exposed me to a wide range of issues in educational technology. The mentoring journey led me closer to my dream of being a technology educator.

CONCLUSION

My case emphasizes both the learning community and mutual benefits features of the faculty mentoring program. As an international student who was relatively new to the graduate program, at the time I first participated in the mentoring program, the community around the program was especially significant to me. All of the relationships in this community helped me to develop both my skills and my confidence. Although both of the faculty members I mentored were clear about the value of the program for them, my story emphasizes the value of the program for me. Through this program, I had the opportunity to interact closely with two highly skilled education professors and to share their thinking about pedagogy and student learning. I also saw that they valued my help and respected my expertise. Through the experience, I felt that I became a valued member of all parts of the technology learning community described in Figure 5.3.

As a result of this initial mentoring program, I chose faculty development as my major research interest in my doctoral program and I went on to conduct my dissertation research on this topic. In the future, I will work to apply the basic approach of this program to faculty development in Taiwan, and I am optimistic about the possibility of making this type of program work within my own culture.

REFERENCES

Bandura, A. (1977). *Self-efficacy: The exercise of control.* New York: W.H. Freeman.

Carroll, T. G. (2000). If we didn't have the schools we have today, would we create the schools we have today? *Contemporary Issues in Technology and Teacher Education* [Online serial], *1*(1). Retrieved February 15, 2003, from http://www.citejournal.org/vol1/iss1/currentissues/general/article1.htm.

Dewey, J. (1966). *Democracy and education: An introduction to the philosophy of education.* New York: Free Press.

Rogoff, B., Matusov, E., & White, C. (1996). Models of teaching and learning: Participation in a community of learners. In D. R. Olson, & N. Torrance (Eds.). *The handbook of education and human development: New models of learning, teaching and schooling* (pp. 388–414). Oxford, England: Blackwell Publishers, Inc.

Rogers, E. M. (2003). *Diffusion of innovations* (5th ed.). New York, NY: Free Press.

Sergiovanni, T. J. (1994). *Building community in schools.* San Francisco: Jossey-Bass.

Vygotsky, L.S. (1978). *Mind in society.* Cambridge, MA: Harvard University Press.

CHAPTER 6

DESIGNING AN ON-LINE LEARNING ENVIRONMENT

Experts Learning Together

Qian Li

This case study features a faculty member in the Department of Curriculum and Instruction at Iowa State University who decided to integrate emerging technologies into a traditional distance education course that is taught on campus as well as off campus via a video-link to remote sites. Specifically, this faculty member wanted to use the WebCT software to strengthen her instruction and class interaction. This faculty member faced two major challenges when integrating technology into teaching, as do most faculty members. First, she needed just-in-time technical support in order to use technology efficiently. Secondly, she needed a clear vision of the use of available technology tools to enhance the teaching and learning process. The faculty member who became my mentee decided to take on the challenges of integrating an emerging technology into her course design and changing her teaching style. The faculty technology mentoring program helped create a special bond between a technology savvy student mentor and the faculty mentee. This special bond allowed the faculty member to obtain needed technical support in a nonthreatening way and to view technology integration from a student's perspective. This collaboration creates a knowledge base for the faculty mentee, the first and most

Faculty Mentoring: The Power of Students in Developing Technology Expertise, pages 71–77

important step of Rogers' innovation-decision process, as she was provided a how-to and know-why technology integration experience.

FACULTY MENTEE PROFILE

Dr. Rosenbusch is an associate professor in the Department of Curriculum and Instruction. She is also the director of the National K–12 Foreign Languages Resource Center (http://www.educ.iastate.edu/nflrc/). Dr. Rosenbusch was already familiar with distance education during this study. She taught an undergraduate course, Methods in Foreign Language Instruction: Elementary School (CI 468), over the Iowa Communication Network (ICN). The ICN is an agency that administers a statewide fiber optic network. Off-campus students interacted with the instructor and the on-campus students during the scheduled class periods via the ICN and used U.S. mail and fax machines to submit assignments.

Dr. Rosenbusch was interested in using technology in this class. She was an intermediate computer user with a positive attitude toward technology. She was already confident and comfortable using computers. She handled e-mail via Eudora, searched the Internet, organized and managed documents using MS Word, created simple PowerPoint presentations, recorded students' grades via computer, and used WebCT to support some of her classroom teaching. She expressed enthusiasm about integrating technology into her courses.

Dr. Rosenbusch wanted to design a WebCT site, which would facilitate class discussion and also allow students to access course information quickly and easily. Her mentoring goals included:

1. to become familiar with a new version of WebCT; and
2. to build a course site to assist her teaching of Methods in Foreign Language Instruction: Elementary School (CI 468).

STUDENT MENTOR PROFILE

I was in the second year of my Master's degree program in instructional technology when I joined the faculty technology mentoring program. Previously, I earned a B.A in English in China and taught English as a foreign language to college students at a university in Beijing. In 1999, I came to the United States and began graduate work in educational technology. My motivation and interest in this field stemmed from my belief that technology can improve productivity and effectiveness in teaching and learning. My technology experience included the use of computer software programs such as Microsoft Office, Dreamweaver, Claris Homepage, WebCT, Adobe Photoshop, and Macromedia Director. I also learned instructional design principles and theories during my program of study.

When I heard about the mentoring program, I signed up immediately for Technology in Teacher Education (CI610). I believed that the mentoring experience would enable me to work closely with a faculty member, to see how a subject matter expert designed a course, and how instructional technology fit into it. I expected the mentoring experience to push me to refine and deepen my computer skills as I proceeded with the mentoring tasks.

LEARNING ABOUT WEBCT 3.0

In our first mentoring meeting, Dr. Rosenbusch and I clarified the mentoring goals. As supported in Social Learning Theory (Rogers, 2003), this mutual and clear goal setting played an important role in guiding our mentoring sessions and meeting Dr. Rosenbusch's needs and expectations. We would focus on learning WebCT 3.0 and building an online platform for her students to access class information and course discussions. We set up every Monday for one hour in the afternoon for our mentoring meetings and laid out a working agenda for the entire semester.

Since Dr. Rosenbusch and I both used WebCT 1.3, we were not worried about learning a new version. We thought that learning the new version was going to be a smooth update of skills. However, we were wrong. After we looked at the new WebCT, we were troubled by some major changes in the interface. We couldn't apply much of what we already knew about the old WebCT to the new one. Old, familiar terms had changed. I was not able to give clear guidance without first learning and trying the program by myself. Dr. Rosenbusch seemed uncomfortable with the new WebCT too, because she couldn't find the buttons and areas to perform her familiar tasks such as adding students to courses and uploading or downloading files. Fortunately, our positive attitude saved us and encouraged us. Rogers (2003) describes attitude as an important factor that affects the adoption of an innovation. Rogers also suggests that the interpersonal communication channels established by Dr. Rosenbusch and myself are very helpful in decreasing the uncertainty about the innovation outcomes. We encouraged each other and decided to learn the new WebCT version. Dr. Rosenbusch said that she would not be so "easily frustrated." She found some related workshops on campus to attend and I spent some time exploring WebCT with the help of an on-line tutorial.

The next several mentoring meetings went smoothly. We created a list of steps to try on the new WebCT each mentoring session. For example, we attempted to customize a page, add a content module, and create a discussion section during one of our mentoring meetings. Gradually, we began to accomplish simple tasks, such as adding WebCT tools, adding icons, and changing page layouts. Sometimes I showed her how to do a certain step and other times Dr. Rosenbusch showed me how to do things. It was an enjoyable experience of sharing. When we got stuck, we encouraged each other by saying, "it doesn't matter, and we will figure it out." We called or e-mailed technical staff in the University Instructional Technology Center for help or simply tried again next time. We were like partners, working together to use WebCT. Gradually, our anxiety and stress level regarding the new WebCT waned.

DESIGNING AND DEVELOPING ON-LINE LEARNING ENVIRONMENTS ON WEBCT 3.0

Though we were far from proficient, we decided to start our project of constructing Methods in Foreign Language Instruction: Elementary School (CI 468) on the new WebCT. Although I had previously completed some instructional design courses and had designed some on-line lesson units for class projects, a complete course on WebCT 3.0 was new for me. I was also unfamiliar with the course content of CI 468. Dr. Rosenbusch explained the course goals and objectives, content, outline, delivery, and assessment to me. Thus, I had a good understanding of her course. We brainstormed ideas to integrate technology into her course design, such as using short video clips and starting a discussion forum for students to reflect on their readings. After this decision was made, we began to implement our ideas as we stepped into the implementation stage to practice the innovation. Sahin, in Chapter 2, describes that the mentor's social reinforcements and technical assistance help the mentee overcome obstacles and effectively integrate technology into teaching. The following section describes the process and the results of a successful implementation of the innovation.

One dilemma Dr. Rosenbusch faced was her temptation to put everything on-line. She tended to simply convert the whole course pack of material into a web version with WebCT. She showed me the course pack and asked me about how she could scan each page and put them into WebCT. I realized that was a common problem of faculty in designing on-line courses. They are not familiar with the strengths of different media. I worried about this approach, because I knew it wouldn't work well! However, I was not sure how to address the issue. I brought it to our CI 610 class for discussion. It was wonderful to have this group to talk about problems, generate ideas, and share resources. Both my classmates and the instructor helped me to analyze my problem and provided suggestions. Then, in the following mentoring meeting, I followed the advice from the CI 610 class and asked Dr. Rosenbusch to visualize what might happen if everything were on-line. We started a list of "what ifs" from the perspective of her students. After some discussion, Dr. Rosenbusch realized that putting everything on-line would only produce an "electronic page turner" and that the purpose of technology was to enrich and enhance her instruction instead of simply serving as an alternative delivery method. She then identified which course material should be on-line and how each medium, such as printed material and the web, complemented each other. She began to consider the impact of visuals, graphics, and multimedia components on WebCT and the use of Discussions, Chat, and Mail functions in WebCT to supplement her course. It was a challenge for her to think of teaching differently with WebCT rather than lecturing in a face-to-face classroom. Though she was enthusiastic about technology integration, she struggled to learn the strength of the web and to adjust to the on-line learning environment.

In order to help Dr. Rosenbusch become familiar with the on-line learning environment, I shared the WebCT sites of other faculty members with her. This proved to be very effective. Those web sites were live models that allowed her to see how her colleagues were teaching in an on-line environment. We discussed online instructional activities. She quickly saw ways to use similar Internet activities with her students using the discussion bulletin board. She became interested in including more class activities on WebCT, because she felt that those activities were doable and manageable. She realized that the role of an instructor in an on-line learning environment was that of a facilitator.

After viewing some examples, we started a rough storyboard on paper. I explained to Dr. Rosenbusch why we needed a storyboard and how to create one. We used the program Inspiration to design the storyboard. The storyboard was helpful in making our project and its outcomes more visible to Dr. Rosenbusch, providing observability for the innovation. Hence, this process helped us clarify our ideas about navigation and gave us a sense of the web site layout. During later mentoring meetings, Dr. Rosenbusch always kept the storyboard beside her and referred to it from time to time.

The final step was to produce what we had designed on paper on the new WebCT. It was a challenging task. Dr. Rosenbusch controlled the mouse to do the work. Sometimes she got stuck, and I waited for her to try to solve the problem herself. If needed, I probed with questions to help her recall the right procedures. If we ran into issues we could not solve, we sought help from technical support personnel in the University's Instructional Technology Center and the Center for Technology in Learning and Teaching. After sitting down together and trying to find appropriate terms

Figure 6.1. Dr. Rosenbusch's WebCT course site.

to communicate our difficulties, we sent e-mails or made calls to technical support personnel.

By the end of the semester, Dr. Rosenbusch reached her goal of building the basic structure of a course on WebCT with discussions, mail, and content modules on the site (see Figure 6.1). She became familiar with uploading and downloading files by herself. She gradually began independently performing tasks on WebCT, such as converting files to html, and uploading files to WebCT. Because of a conflict in finals week, I couldn't meet with her for our last mentoring session. She said that she would work on WebCT by herself and let me know if she had any problems. This gave her another opportunity to overcome her anxiety of using WebCT. I told her to e-mail me if she needed help. The next day, I received the e-mail message that indicated she was successful. She said that she was thrilled that she made it! As Babcock mentiones in Chapter 9, our experience also showed that the individual-centered approach of the mentoring program was very effective in encouraging faculty to use instructional technologies independently.

CONCLUSION

Similar to the experience Chuang describes in Chapter 5, the theme of mutual benefit is strong in my mentoring story. It is hard for me to say which one of us learned more. The shared learning nature of this experience really made my mentoring dynamic and rewarding. Dr. Rosenbusch was satisfied with her experience and continued to use technology in her teaching environment. She was happy to learn the potential for using WebCT to facilitate her teaching. At the same time, she began to understand how to adjust her instructional style, and even pedagogy, to make the best use of an on-line teaching environment.

I also benefited greatly from the mentoring experience. I became familiar with the WebCT 3.0 program and used it to design an online learning environment. With Dr. Rosenbusch, I reviewed different ideas about technology integration into teaching and further explored and evaluated the application of WebCT in her specific subject area. Involvement in the course design process enabled me to understand the obstacles involved for faculty in technology integration.

In addition, mentoring increased my ability to communicate with technical people. I acted in the role of technology coordinator for Dr. Rosenbusch, connecting her with the technology core group of the department and the university. I learned many technical terms in order to explain technical questions and answers with technology support personnel. When I asked for help for the first time, I was uncertain and hesitant. Now I am confident of my proficiency in communicating my ideas accurately and intelligently with technical people.

Finally, as an international student the mentoring program was an excellent opportunity for me to understand the teaching and learning culture in American universities. By working closely with Dr. Rosenbusch, I saw how an American faculty member organized her teaching, designed her class activities, and evaluated student learning. I also learned her beliefs about the teaching and learning process. It is quite clear that one of the major features of my case is that I benefited from the experience as much, if not more, than Dr. Rosenbusch.

REFERENCE

Rogers, E. M. (2003). *Diffusion of innovations* (5th ed.). New York, NY: Free Press.

CHAPTER 7

UNDERSTANDING AND ADDRESSING A FACULTY MEMBER'S CONCERNS IN THE TECHNOLOGY INTEGRATION PROCESS

Sonmez Pamuk

This case study explores a two semester technology mentoring relationship between a faculty member, Dr. Smith, senior special education faculty member in the Department of Curriculum and Instruction at Iowa State University (ISU) and me, a graduate student in the Department of Curriculum and Instruction. The main focus of this case is to describe specific experiences with the process of technology integration into teaching exhibited by Dr. Smith with my help. The events that took place in the mentoring meetings are examined based on the Concerns Based Adoption Model (CBAM) of Hall and Hord (1987). Although Rogers' model is the main theoretical framework for this book (Chapter 2), and illustrates mentoring experiences from both the individual and the system perspectives, CBAM puts more emphasis on the understanding of individuals' concerns in the process of the adoption of an innovation (Ellsworth, 2000). As a mentor I didn't want to just meet with Dr. Smith and give him some instructions on his technology needs, but I also wanted to use my own experience and knowledge on the subject to encourage him to think

Faculty Mentoring: The Power of Students in Developing Technology Expertise, pages 79–91

about new and effective ways to integrate technology into his teaching. Thus, I found that CBAM provides a very clear framework that describes steps that I needed to take, including how to raise his awareness of a new technological idea and to help him develop the necessary skills to adopt it. Another important factor that played a key role in using CBAM in this case was that I wanted to know how well I was addressing and assisting him in this process of mentoring, and the CBAM stages of concern can provide evidence of progress. This chapter begins with both mentor and mentee profiles and proceeds with details of mentoring meetings and the connection between the CBAM and our mentoring relationship.

THE MENTOR PROFILE

I am a doctoral student in the Curriculum and Instructional Technology program at ISU. My research interests are in teacher education and issues in teacher education related to the use of technology. I participated in the technology mentoring course for the first time in fall of 2002. In fall 2004, I worked as a graduate research assistant in the course and assumed leadership responsibilities. I presented technical workshops on topics of interest to the mentors and helped Dr. Thompson with the implementation of the course. As part of my leadership in the course, I was paired with Dr. Smith, who had volunteered to work with a mentor for about one hour each week. During this pairing process, I was also informed that Dr. Smith would like to work on a variety of technology applications based on the technology mentor's expertise and his own needs. His first priority was working on WebCT. Dr. Thompson and I decided that working with a mentee would be helpful in my leadership role in the class, as I would be sharing mentoring experiences with students in the class. I had previously taken the class as a graduate student in 2002, and this would be my second faculty mentoring experience.

After working with Dr. Smith for several months (two semesters), I have come to think that this initial pairing process, as mentioned by Thompson earlier, was one of the most important and foremost factors which shaped the nature (professional, respectful, and mutually beneficial) of my mentoring relationship with Dr. Smith and motivated me to work with him in following semesters. I found that, not only were my technology skills well-matched with Dr. Smith's needs, but that our personalities were also well-matched.

I began the mentoring relationship with Dr. Smith with relatively advanced skills using a variety of technologies (word processing, spreadsheets, web designing, video conferencing tools, knowledge of open source applications, etc.). Thus my major initial interest in the mentoring relationship with Dr. Smith was the expectation that this experience would help me to develop a deeper understanding of how a teacher education faculty member might use technology to support their teaching.

THE MENTEE PROFILE

Dr. Smith is a professor of Special Education in the Department of Curriculum and Instruction at Iowa State University. After working for several years in a division of special education for the State Department of Education and with other universities, he had recently joined the ISU teacher education program. He was teaching his first graduate class at ISU when we began working together.

After meeting with Dr. Smith, he expressed his initial plan of using an online course management system (e.g. WebCT, Blackboard) to supplement his face-to-face class sessions. He had had some experience with the Blackboard environment at another institution and was interested in expanding his ability to use online course tools. He had been using the general applications that most other faculty members use in their professional and personal activities: electronic mail, Internet, Microsoft PowerPoint, and Microsoft Word. He had these software programs installed on his Macintosh laptop, which was connected to the one desktop monitor in his office.

MENTORING MEETINGS

In our first mentoring meeting, Dr. Smith and I talked about what he wanted to work on throughout the semester and tried to establish some goals to accomplish through our mentoring meetings. Sahin discusses in Chapter 2 that having some goals established based on the mentee's needs helps to create a collaborative learning environment for both mentor and mentee which ultimately supports their learning. Based on Dr. Smith's needs, we decided to start working with WebCT immediately because the semester had already started and Dr. Smith was teaching his first face-to-face graduate course at ISU. He had already done some of the PowerPoint presentations for his class when we met, so our first task was to make these presentations available to his students so that they could access them if they missed the class or wanted to reuse them at their own pace.

In this first meeting, my feelings about my relationship with Dr. Smith were very different than they were at the end of the semester. In the first meeting, I was not only nervous about meeting a faculty member, but I was also nervous about helping him with technology. First, I was conscious of the fact that as an international graduate student, I had limited experience in the American education system. Second, I was aware that we were working in a content area, special education, in which I had little background. International student mentors seem to face more challenges due to cultural differences when first entering the mentor program as Chuang also mentions in Chapter 5. Many international students, like me, come from countries where the hierarchy of the student/teacher relationship is emphasized. Thus, even introducing oneself to a faculty member as a mentor seemed a bit presumptuous. But after introducing ourselves, Dr. Smith sent the first explicit sign that our relationship was not going to be overly formal. Instead, we would have an informal professional relationship that would provide me with a chance to observe the issues that a faculty member experiences in learning and integrating technology. It was also clear that we would have an environment where I would be able to share my own ideas about using technology in teaching and learning and possibly the opportunity to test some of these ideas in a real classroom setting.

I don't know if he already understood my feelings, or if he was excited about learning about my background and culture. His "*tell me about...*" questions about myself, my country, family, and the education system in my country during our first meeting were very effective in lowering my anxiety and setting up our initial informal and undeclared relationship protocol. Rogers' (2003) model, as discussed by Sahin in detail in Chapter 2, stresses the importance of interpersonal communication channels in the innovation adoption process. According to this model, interpersonal communication is effective in dealing with resistance to an innovation. Hence, I found that our first meeting played a crucial role for establishing this open communication channel between Dr. Smith and myself. It would not only reduce his resistance to innovative ideas, but also would help me overcome my anxieties as an international student and become more confident and effective in the mentoring process.

In our undeclared relationship protocol, there was an immediate sign of mutual respect and benefit. Dr. Smith indicated that he valued my need to benefit from the experience by asking me, "*Ok, I'm expecting to learn these things from you. How about you? How do these meetings benefit you? Do I need to do anything?*" Chuang, Thompson, and Schmidt in Chapter 3 describe this attention to shared benefits I experienced as "one element of successful mentoring." Dr. Smith made it clear that he, as a faculty member, was concerned with my learning from the mentoring relationship and that he viewed the relationship as far more than just having a graduate student who shares information with him.

A few minutes into our first meeting, we immediately took the first concrete step of requesting his first WebCT on-line course from the Information Technology Center at the University through a Web based request form. During the first meeting, we also talked about the functionality of the technology he had: a cell phone, a Macintosh laptop, and a Palm Pilot. All of these technologies were the latest models; his cell phone had a camera, his Palm Pilot had the ability to connect to the Internet, and he had a recently released laptop. However, Dr. Smith had not used any of these technologies, especially his Palm Pilot and cell phone, for any advanced purpose. He was limited to very basic functions such as talking on the phone, or checking his schedule on the Palm Pilot. His aspirations to learn and use all the functionalities of these technology pieces were obvious. One day, he put his cell phone and Palm Pilot by the laptop on his office desk and said "*... I would like to use all of these [cell phone, palm pilot and the laptop] more than I use them now.*"

From the beginning of our relationship, in our conversations, I tried to support my ideas about any specific technology use with the real examples from the field or literature. For instance, when I indicated that the cell phone with a camera feature could be used effectively for educational purposes, I followed by saying that Dr. X uses it for taking pictures in the field and then she shows the pictures to students or puts the pictures on-line in her WebCT site. My intention was not only to help Dr. Smith in learning or memorizing steps to complete the task through a "how to" type approach but also to bring him new ideas and persuade him to use them in his teaching. Our later meetings proved that bringing real examples from the field was a very relevant and appropriate strategy to show him the possibilities available when using technology and to encourage him to generate more ideas about how to use technology in his teaching.

In following meetings, after we had his WebCT site created, we started working on developing the WebCT site together. Dr. Smith wanted to put his syllabus and PowerPoint presentations on-line. In these meetings, there was an undeclared "do not touch the mouse" rule between us. Except for a few occasions, Dr. Smith designed the WebCT site by himself. In the beginning of the design process, I gave him a short introduction about WebCT, its interface, and general rules for designers. We added his students, as the first step, to the WebCT site so that they would be able to access the site, and then we made a Microsoft Word copy of his syllabus and converted it into a html file format for WebCT. Then we uploaded it to WebCT. This process of uploading the syllabus and PowerPoint presentations to WebCT took us more than three meeting sessions. At the earlier stages of this process, the nature of the relationship was a very traditional training program format. I was telling him what to do and how to do it, and he was following me and taking some notes on his small notebook about the steps we took. However, toward the end of the process, he wanted to be more active in doing things alone and said "*OK, let me go through how to upload my PowerPoint presentation for this week to the WebCT, and if I do need help, I'll ask.*" By following his notes, he took almost all necessary steps to complete the task with very little help from me. I was also encouraged that our relationship had developed to the point where he was comfortable setting new rules for how we would proceed with the uploading.

In addition to designing Dr. Smith's WebCT site in our weekly meetings, we also spent time talking about different ideas and their possible impacts on his teaching. One of the ideas that I was encouraging was the use of video clips in his teaching. When I first introduced him to this idea, as noted earlier, I supported my idea by explaining my preference as a student:

> Dr. Smith, for example, don't you think that it would be more powerful to show a case coming from a K–12 school classroom and ask your students to discuss it rather than giving them a paper that describes the case? As a student, I would strongly prefer to have the video clips...

He agreed and liked the idea of using video clips in teaching and for his other academic endeavors, such as presenting at conferences. In later weeks, after we were finished with the WebCT site, at Dr. Smith's request I talked about how we could create the video clips in general terms and explained the process that we needed to go through: importing videos from one resource to the computer, converting them from analog format to digital ones, and so on. The week after we first discussed video clips, we met in his office as usual and went to the Center for Technology in Learning and Teaching (CTLT). The CTLT is located in the lower level of the building and is very well equipped with the latest computers, camcorders, recorders, and VHS players. Since we needed a VHS player connected to the computer with a digitizer, we used the facilities available at the CTLT. In addition to the technical facilities at the center, I also wanted to introduce the center to him because the CTLT is not just a center for technology but also the center of the community that connects the novice and advanced users of different technologies. Thus, I thought that the CTLT would also be a good resource for Dr. Smith where he could get help from the CTLT service employees (graduate and undergraduate students) at any time he needed help. Before the fall semester was over, we were able to create his first two video clips from two different movie VHS tapes, and we copied them onto CDs. However, Dr. Smith didn't have time to use them in class in that first semester that we worked together.

Although Dr. Smith didn't have time to use the video clips in the classroom that semester, he e-mailed me during the winter break and asked about the video clips that we created. Although we were working on the WebCT site for Dr. Smith's graduate course when I first introduced him to the idea of using video clips so that his graduate students would become more active in WebCT, he wanted use these clips for an undergraduate class and for assessment purposes. Because of our positive relationship, I was happy to continue working with him voluntarily on his needs as much as possible. This continuation of the mentoring relationship beyond the "required" semester is typical theme in the program. Like Dr. Smith and I, many mentors and mentees choose to continue their work together after the required course experience is finished. Since I felt that I was learning as much as Dr. Smith from the experience, continuing the relationship was mutually beneficial.

During the second semester of our relationship, I met with him twice in the first week to create his WebCT class site and assisted him in embedding the video clips into PowerPoint. In addition, we checked to ensure that the video clips work with PowerPoint. Finally, we checked that his laptop worked with the classroom's projector. During the second semester of our relationship we met, biweekly or so, based on his needs and time schedule. In the second semester, Dr. Smith had moved one step ahead by creating a "digital video clip" library to use in future activities. We had decided to meet and create more clips for the summer semester. Although Dr. Smith didn't use video cases much in that time period, we worked together and developed materials for the future. Rogers (2003) describes the process Dr. Smith and I went through as typical stages in an innovation adoption. According to Rogers, as presented in Chapter 2, an innovation adoption includes newly perceived ideas that result in any favorable or unfavorable attitude change toward innovation.

In the second semester of our mentoring meetings, Dr. Smith was more confident and independent compared to our earlier meetings in learning and working with WebCT and the other technologies. However, it was obvious that Dr. Smith still needed time and assistance to continue using WebCT and other applications with more advanced functions.

CONCERNS BASED ADOPTION MODEL AND OUR MENTORING RELATIONSHIP

As many studies have reported, any plan intended to make change on an individual or in an organization takes time and requires ongoing support. Thus, change is described not as a short time event but a process (Hall & Hord, 1987; Ellsworth, 2000; Fullan, 2001). In our case, I viewed the whole case as a change process of a faculty member on his approach and ideas about the use of technology in teaching rather than teaching technology to him in a short period of time. Conversations between the two of us, the projects that we worked on, and our learning in different subjects including different technologies and pedagogy, were some of the pieces of the change that took place for both of us. Since this case mainly focuses on understanding the innovation adoption process of Dr. Smith and his developing levels of concern about technology integration, I chose to use CBAM as a framework to describe and explain his process of change. Thus I will now describe how the technology mentoring relationship was effective in understanding and addressing Dr. Smith's concerns about technology integration as well as his approach to "innovative ideas" using principles of the CBAM framework.

The Concern Based Adoption Model of Hall and Hord (1987) is a model that provides us with a framework to understand the dynamics and facilitation of the change process in the adoption of an innovation. The CBAM consists of three dynamics: (1) stages of concern, (2) level of use and (3) innovation configuration. One of the most important premises of this model for successful change process is to know how well the change facilitator understands the innovation user's attitudes and concerns about the innovation and how quickly and appropriately he or she addresses them. Hence, the authors put much emphasis on the "stages of concerns" in the framework. They conclude that the consideration of the innovation user's concerns is the key factor for a successful change. In addition to the importance of the stages of concerns in the CBAM framework, Hall and Hord (1987) point out that assessment of "level of use" in the model is difficult and requires the researcher to use an "intensive observational approach" to collect reliable data not just from the classroom setting, but from other environments where the innovation user will be. Given the importance of the innovation adopter's levels of concern and the opportunity to collect data from Dr. Smith's experiences for an entire year, I chose to analyze my case from the perspective of stages of concern.

Stages of Concerns

According to the model (Table 7.1), there are seven different stages of concern that the innovation intended adopter may have: *awareness, informational, personal, management, consequence, collaboration, and refocusing.*

Hord and Hall (1987) suggest that the knowledge of these stages can help the change facilitator (graduate student mentor) understand what stage the given individual, a faculty member (Dr. Smith), is in the change process (Ellsworth, 2000). With this understanding, the mentor can help support and guide the mentee through these stages. In my mentoring relationship with Dr. Smith, I saw several instances of how Dr. Smith progressed through these stages of concern. In each project, we had to go through the cycle of stages of concern several times. For example, Dr. Smith had already identified his need for WebCT when we began the mentoring process. In this case, he was aware of the WebCT (awareness), had some information about it (informational) through his own experience and from his

Table 7.1. Stages of Concern in CBAM

Awareness	has little concern about or involvement with the innovation
Informational	has a general awareness of the innovation and interest in learning some details of it.
Personal	has some questions about his or her abilities to meet the demands of the innovation; his or her role with the innovation.
Management	has concerns about the processes and tasks of using the innovation, best use of information resources and some issues related to how much time, effort etc. that he or she needs to put into learning and using the innovation.
Consequence	has concerns about the effectiveness and benefits of the innovation to his or her students.
Collaboration	seeks collaboration with his or her peers, colleagues and some other users of the innovation.
Refocusing	generates new ideas to make the innovation more beneficial or finds more effective alternatives to replace it.

colleagues in the college, and he understood some of the limitations in using it. To me, Dr. Smith had already initiated the change process by himself and experienced the first three stages of concern (awareness, informational, and personal). However, with the new knowledge and practice he gained, we came through the same stages with other specific applications of WebCT at points during our meetings. For example, when we were designing Dr. Smith's course in WebCT, we had conversations on how an on-line discussion board would be used for his class. As a student, I shared my experiences with discussion boards. He started asking me how we could use a discussion board and shared his ideas about the possible benefits for him and his students. He was seeking more details and a clear understanding of using WebCT discussion boards. For this reason, we went back to the first stages and discussed what WebCT discussion boards actually were and how they would be beneficial to him and to his students. As we went through the first three stages (awareness, informational, personal) together, he already had some ideas and I addressed some of his concerns during our sessions by giving some information to him about WebCT discussion boards.

After a few practice sessions, Dr. Smith began to use WebCT in his class and then faced some real issues coming from his students about his WebCT course. He wanted to address his students' problems (accessing WebCT, e-mailing in WebCT, etc.) as quickly as possible in the classroom. These real and emergent student issues pushed him to move forward to the next stage (management) on the CBAM and he expressed a strong desire to spend time with me to address management concerns. From our conversations during our regular meeting time and his "…if you happen to be on campus and have a minute stop by" e-mails, I knew that my availability to assist him at this stage as was very critical. Without the just-in-time support provided from the mentoring program, I believe that Dr. Smith's management concerns might have been overwhelming and might have caused him to give up on the use of WebCT.

Of course, Dr. Smith did not just bring his concerns about learning and using WebCT to the mentoring meetings. We also had several conversations on how WebCT would help his students. Throughout our mentoring meetings, students' benefits were one of the key components of our work. Dr. Smith and I both worked to determine how we could use technology so that the students in his classroom would be more engaged and motivated to learn. CBAM describes this pattern of behaviors exhibited by Dr. Smith as the "consequence" stage. In this stage, according to the model, the innovation user demonstrates concerns about the benefits of the innovation to his or her students. Having a partner to discuss with and problem solve through this stage of concern seemed to be very useful to Dr. Smith.

During the second semester of our mentoring meetings together, Dr. Smith was clearly more comfortable using some WebCT functions. One day he asked me, "tell me how other faculty members in the mentoring program use WebCT differently." I got the impression that Dr. Smith was indeed looking for some collaboration with his colleagues at the college to improve and advance his use of WebCT and that he was moving to the collaboration stage in the model. As an example of his collaboration efforts, he mentioned that he had some conversations with his colleagues at ISU and other institutions on potential uses of WebCT and other technologies. In addition, he was brainstorming on the idea of delivering some of the courses in his program entirely on-line with the help from one of his colleagues who was involved in similar projects at his institution. This process, according to him, would possibly require extensive use of WebCT, videoconferencing and some other technologies. In terms of the "refocusing" stage in the model, Dr. Smith had plans for the new semester (Fall 2005) to develop some ways in which he could integrate more interactions with all of his students throughout the semester and intended to move to a "virtually paperless class." I was pleased as Dr. Smith moved into these stages since CBAM theory stresses that the consequence, collaboration and refocusing stages become more intense when the person becomes more experienced and skilled with the innovation.

When Dr. Smith became more confident using WebCT features, he decided to work on using video clips for his undergraduate class as a piece of an on-line quiz that he wanted to administer. This on-line quiz featuring a video clip was one of the ideas that we had discussed more than four months before the implementation, but, as previously described, it took several months to begin and we ended up using the video clip for a different purpose than intended. Since we had already created two short clips in the previous semester, he was thinking that they were ready to use, but actually they were not. The video files' sizes were too large to upload to WebCT. In response to his concerns about using these video clips, I introduced the possibility of streaming video to him. I also told him about some resources on campus to make video clips files smaller with different player formats so that students would be able to open them with Windows Media Player, Realtime Player, and others.

Based on these scenes from my experience with Dr. Smith, the pattern that Dr. Smith followed in his technology learning and implementation process was directly tied to the relationship between his concerns about the technology piece (WebCT and others) and how I addressed those concerns. Adequate information motivated him to think about the benefits of using the technology that I proposed. As he practiced, he became more comfortable using technology and he sought alternative ideas and technologies for teaching.

Overall, when I look over the pattern of concerns that Dr. Smith exhibited and the approaches we used to address these concerns throughout our mentoring relationship from the CBAM perspective, I found that each task we worked on had its own stages of concern that we had to go through. In each transition from one task to another, such as learning a new feature of WebCT, we started the new cycle of "stages of concern" again for the new task and spent time addressing some of his concerns about what the new task was, what we needed to know, how to complete the task, and how it would work.

While we moved between these stages of concern for each task, I noticed that there was a strong interwoven relationship between some of Dr. Smith's concerns and his ability to use the technology piece on which we were working. Because of this existing relationship, Dr. Smith's understanding of the process of what we needed to do and how to do it was not enough to proceed to the next task in our plan. Thus, I felt, as a mentor that I needed to give special attention to Dr. Smith's practicing and developing necessary skills to use technology. To do so, we spent more time and effort addressing some of his management-type concerns rather than the personal or informational stage concerns. For instance, for Dr. Smith's immediate needs, he needed to learn how to upload the course syllabus and the PowerPoint presentation to his WebCT course site. As mentioned earlier, we spent several weeks practicing those tasks.

To me, developing competence was a very critical point in terms of motivating him to be more active and eager to seek the other possibilities available. As I observed Dr. Smith's WebCT progress, it was obvious that he didn't want to move forward until he felt comfortable using that specific feature. In a more specific format, as Dr. Smith became more confident that he was able to upload his PowerPoint file to WebCT by himself, he then said, "OK...Let's check the other things."

CONCLUSION

For this mentoring case, CBAM theory provided a useful lens for understanding and encouraging the faculty development process. In order to provide more appropriate assistance for Dr. Smith on his technology needs, I needed to find out the issues and concerns about the technologies he needed and then determine whether or not I was using the appropriate strategies to address them. In our early meetings, Dr. Smith and I mostly worked on his immediate, and predetermined technology needs (i.e. WebCT). The CBAM provided me, as mentor, useful guidance to identify his position in terms of what he knew about the chosen technology, how well he was using it, and what he needed to know about and practice with it. As we continued to work, and Dr. Smith became more fluent in using these technologies, we had more conversations on different ideas and technologies. In these conversations, I used CBAM's stages of concerns to introduce new ideas (for example, the use of video clips) to him that I thought would be useful in his teaching.

Thus, for both understanding and addressing Dr. Smith's needs and introducing new ideas, I found that the CBAM framework was very appropriate for our work together. Through the Faculty Technology Mentoring Program, I was able to provide assistance and support as he worked through the levels of concern in adopting an innovation. I noticed that we tended to re-visit each stage of concern as we worked with new and different technology applications. Our story provides evidence that just-in-time, personal support was helpful for addressing his concerns and in encouraging his adoption of technology in his teaching. Although it is clear that Dr. Smith is just beginning in his journey through the change process, I have evidence that he has started down the road of change and will continue the process. He was very clear about his interest in continuing our mentoring relationship and his desire to expand his use of technology in his special education classes.

REFERENCES

Ellsworth, J. B. (2000). *Surviving change: A survey of educational change models.* Syracuse, NY: ERIC Clearinghouse on Information & Technology.

Fullan, M. (2001). *The new meaning of educational change (3rd ed.).* New York: Teachers College Press.

Hall, E. G. & Hord, M. S. (1987). *Change in schools: Facilitating the process.* Albany, NY: State University of New York Press.
Rogers, E.M. (2003). *Diffusion of Innovations* (5th ed.). New York: Free Press.

CHAPTER 8

TECHNOLOGY MENTORING THROUGH THE EYES OF K–5 PRACTITIONERS

Comfort Kouadio

The case that follows exemplifies an individualized approach to on-the-job, ongoing, professional development in technology-based learning in a K–12 environment. The approach is similar to the other mentoring cases described in this book, but here the case involved a collaboration between two in-service teachers. In Chapter 2, Sahin described this collaboration as an interpersonal communication channel, according to Rogers' theory, and expressed the importance of this collaboration in the integration of technology in teaching. This teacher-to-teacher sharing and support resulted in a renewed enthusiasm for teaching and for having students engaged in authentic hands-on experiences with technology. Additionally, the case clearly shows that modeling the use of technology and integrating it into curricula takes time, patience, leadership, administrative support, and a community of learners.

MENTOR'S PROFILE

My interest in technology stems in part from a lack of exposure to it during my childhood in Cameroon, West Africa. As an undergraduate student in

Faculty Mentoring: The Power of Students in Developing Technology Expertise, pages 93–104

Psychology at Mankato State University (now Minnesota State University at Mankato), I began using technology for writing term papers and projects on my Sears electric typewriter. One day I ran out of typewriter ribbon and was forced to use whatever was available to finish my project. That led to my first experience with a computer and opened my eyes to the world of more efficient technology.

The next step in my education was choosing Iowa State University for graduate study. At first, I was frustrated to learn that all papers were to be done on a word processor. However, my assistantship in the Department of Curriculum and Instruction provided additional exposure to computers and new interactions with software applications and e-mail. My experiences with technology allowed me to develop age- and ability-appropriate activities aimed at accommodating the diverse needs of my K–5 students. Working with young children pushed me to continually look for ways to enhance their learning.

One way of enhancing their learning was to share my technology-use expertise with a colleague. This sharing came in the form of a mentor-mentee relationship. As a graduate student in the Curriculum and Instruction and Preleadership programs at Iowa State University, I was afforded the opportunity to participate in just such an arrangement. I found the idea of collaborating with another teacher to be both exciting and unique.

MENTEE'S PROFILE

My colleague and mentee was Gwen Rauen with whom I team-taught kindergarten in an inner city school in Des Moines, Iowa. Prior to teaching, she was a practicing nurse. Most of her computer experience had been very specialized and limited, starting when she attended college and continuing while she was working at the Iowa City Care Center, a facility mainly for Alzheimer and cancer patients. It was one of the first facilities of its kind to implement the use of computers for care plans, medical records, doctor's orders, prescription forms, and so forth.

Several other work experiences also involved the use of computer programs specific to nursing or education. The programs were used for things such as billing, building maintenance documentation, creating contracts, and producing written communications between clients. While she was with the West Des Moines Community School District as a special education teacher, she used the computer primarily for e-mail, documentation of safety and medical records, maintenance of specific adaptation plans for disabled students and storage of behavior modification charts. These experiences were, at times, frustrating because of time and availability constraints. Consequently, she enthusiastically spent many hours after work perfecting her computer skills and helping other staff members learn how to use the computer.

Gwen continued her involvement with technology through the purchase of her own personal computer. She spent many hours exploring it and enjoyed learning at her own pace with no pressures or deadlines. She became increasingly familiar with America Online (AOL) for e-mail, and used these applications to communicate with me on an almost daily basis.

Once Gwen started teaching kindergarten, she became a perfect candidate for the type of mentor-mentee collaboration that we initiated. Her interest in, and her exposure to, communication technology and her experience with its use in an educational setting, as well as her level of computer literacy, augured well for her adoption and use of technology-integrated curricula.

TEACHER-TO-TEACHER MENTORING

A variety of forms of staff development facilitate technology learning. Compared with workshops and similar forms of training that Smith & O'Bannon (1999) describe as a "one stop workshop with limited support and follow up for integration," one-on-one, ongoing mentoring seemed to be a promising approach in technology or other learning (Thompson & Schmidt, 1994). This approach was implemented in university as well as in K12 settings.

Overall, research has indicated that teachers are the best teachers of teachers (Marsh, 2000). The idea of "teachers teaching teachers" provides an opportunity to facilitate technology learning. Such an approach, if used consistently, could positively impact teachers' mastery of technology and help integrate technology into the classroom. Locally and nationally, there is a strong concern about the need for technical and financial support to enable teachers to take technology courses and receive on-the-job training through staff development. This concern was emphasized by the American Library Association's (ALA) Presidential Committee on Information Literacy which characterized a literate person as one capable of recognizing information requirements and able to locate, evaluate and effectively use that information. Information in this context included not only the printed word but also media, computer, and network information (Plotnick, 1999).

The National Association for the Education of Young Children (NAEYC) also emphasized the need for increased professional development for teachers in the use of technology. They maintained that professional judgment in the specific uses of technology was a required component of technology integration and added concerns about the role of the teacher in evaluating appropriate uses of technology (NAEYC, 1996). With these concerns and factors in mind, it seems plausible that mentoring might help address the problem. The following section provides an example of such a mentoring approach.

THE MENTORING EXPERIENCE

As a participant in the Iowa State University graduate course "Technology in Teacher Education," I was to serve as a mentor to a colleague. I chose to work with this K–5 colleague because we shared a classroom as an experiment in expanding the mentoring program and because she had expressed interest in learning more about technology integration in the classroom. We met for the first time during the summer. We began to meet on a regular basis both in and out of our school building to discuss and plan for the academic year. These informal meetings enabled us to get to know each other better, a prerequisite for establishing a good working relationship.

As a result of my interest in technology, part of our discussion was about using technology as a tool to support teaching and learning. As a classroom teacher, mentoring a colleague in the field was a natural choice. What an opportunity to subtly influence someone through my excitement with technology! After consulting with my professor, I was ready. As mentioned by Sahin in Chapter 2, goal setting is an important part of the collaborative learning on which Social Learning Theory focuses so Gwen and I began our collaboration by establishing the following goals:

1. Become more familiar with the benefits of a computer in the classroom.
2. Learn some short-cuts in navigating on the computer.
3. Have a classroom computer and a printer that are reliable and fast.
4. Learn how to use a scanner.
5. Have computers in the classroom that are accessible to children to use as a center (work station).
6. Have access to the Smart Board to be used for whole group instruction.
7. Learn about spreadsheets and the benefits for classroom teachers.
8. Learn appropriate computer terminology.
9. Learn more about e-mail, attachments, etc.
10. Become comfortable enough with technology skills to help others who may be hesitant to integrate computer technology into teaching and learning.

From the beginning, Gwen was excited and enthusiastic about everything because of her previous exposure to technology. As we began our technology journey, we encountered several roadblocks, major issues that needed to be resolved before we could proceed. Gwen was feeling overwhelmed with the responsibility for a whole classroom. The situation provided an opportunity to discuss realistically the complexities of teaching and what it takes to integrate technology into the curriculum while effectively managing the other responsibilities associated with teaching.

MENTORING ACTIVITIES AND ARTIFACTS

Our first project began shortly after school started in the fall. Our goal was to use technology in developmentally appropriate ways so that it played a significant role in the learning process. We asked the students how they got ready for kindergarten. The students drew pictures and dictated sentences to describe their drawings (See Figures 8.1, 8.2, and 8.3).

Figure 8.1. One student's drawing.

Figure 8.2. Another student's drawing.

Figure 8.3. A third student's drawing.

Figure 8.4. Gwen prepares for school.

Gwen and I took pictures with the digital camera and then showed our students how we prepared for school (see Figure 8.4). Later, the students learned how to use the digital camera to take pictures.

The students took pictures of their drawings to be placed in a slide using *Kid Pix* slide show capabilities. Next, we began learning how to use *Kid Pix*. We took pictures of students with a digital camera and inserted them into a *Kid Pix* slide. We learned and practiced setting up a slide show with students' pictures and continued to insert new pictures of students into the program.

We also took pictures of the students' work with the digital camera, and put these into slides. Later, we added a transition (clapping sound) to all of the students' pictures. I demonstrated using the computer for lesson plans and saved a template on a disk for Gwen. She continued using her personal computer for creating lesson plans, communicating with me, creating name lists and searching the Internet for appropriate kindergarten sites. We shared and discussed information from her searches, and we talked about the appropriateness of the uses of the websites she found for young learners. Gwen reported that she enjoyed being able to use a computer to create quick and attractive headings for student projects and attractive parent letters. We continued creating the slide show until we had enough information and pictures to complete our project, using additional technical assistance from a master teacher at Iowa State University who provided technology assistance in our school as part of a U.S. Department of Education grant program called Preparing Tomorrow's Teachers to use Technology (PT3).

During Open House in the month of September, we shared our slide show with our students and their families. We were pleased that it was such a huge success. We attended the mentor/mentee gathering at Iowa State University one afternoon. In Chapter 2, Sahin highlighted the importance of these large group meetings of the mentoring program in reducing faculty anxiety and uncertainty about instructional technology and its outcomes and having faculty positive attitudes toward the technology that are crucial in the successful adoption and diffusion of technology in teacher education programs. Gwen was introduced to the other mentors and their mentees. She reviewed our goals and spoke about what we were learning and implementing in the classroom. We continued to practice performing various tasks with the computer. Gwen wrote many letters, developed worksheets, lesson plans, student information forms, and record keeping using her personal computer. We used the computer a great deal when we began assessing the students and documenting and preparing for reading groups, conferences, and progress reports. We took additional pictures of the students to use in literacy related activities such as interactive or shared writing, conversation, name writing, and recognition/social skills.

In October, we continued communicating with each other via e-mail. After a field trip to Iowa State University's C.Y. Stephens Auditorium to see Eric Carle's *The Very Hungry Caterpillar* and *The Very Quiet Cricket*, we shared ideas for technology integration. We accessed Eric Carl's website, viewed some of his books and corresponded with him via e-mail. The students dictated the content of the e-mail and asked questions about his life, such as whether or not he had children and how he began writing books about children.

The month of November brought new challenges. As we began to experiment with more ideas on the computer, we had difficulty with computer technology due to slow computers (by the time the computer was ready for us to work our planning time was over) and limited printer options—no color, no ink. We had less time to plan due to schedule changes and other teaching obligations that seemed to increase as the semester went on. Varying and high levels of diversity among students, student abilities, and academic levels increased the amount of time needed to prepare lessons and activities.

During the month of December we continued to prepare lessons using the computer and communicated via e-mail daily. We looked forward to putting together more slide shows, using *Kid Pix* and possibly *iMovie* as the semester progressed.

REFLECTIONS ON THE MENTORING EXPERIENCE

This mentoring experience was mutually beneficial for us. In her reflection on the experience, Gwen indicated that with me as her partner, she learned more about computer technology, its integration in the classroom, and how to make it accessible to children. Our benefits from and experience with the mentoring program were not limited to only technology adoption. We continued to envision future uses of technology in our classroom and modeled the benefits of technology for our colleagues. We became the change agents of technology to show the effective uses of technology to our colleagues and to support teacher change in technology adoption. Our modeling also contributed to the diffusion of technology. Once again, our experience with the mentoring program supported Sahin's statement in Chapter 2 that the mentoring program contributes to both technology adoption and its diffusion. I found the use of technology to be exciting, fun, efficient, and beneficial for Gwen, my students, and myself. The students were excited by computers and loved to experiment and learn with them. Through efforts like this collaboration, I believe that young learners become competent and efficient future technologists.

This rewarding experience also came with some challenges. Sometimes, when two or more people interact, differences in opinions and personalities surface. Due in part to our proximity (teaching side by side), these differences became more obvious over time. The technology mentoring experience was good for us because we learned to be patient with each other, as well as sensitive and trusting.

This experience reinforced my belief in facilitating and supporting learning rather than being a "gate keeper." Gwen initiated what she wanted to learn through a list of goals, while I assumed the role of providing "just-in-time" or ongoing support, including researching additional appropriate hardware/software or other needed support. My colleagues and professor served as valued sources of support via class discussions and group advice on specific issues related to the mentoring relationship.

At times, Gwen and I struggled to have time to meet. Gwen expressed her frustration with having too many things to juggle. In dealing with this issue, the group's suggestions during our weekly CI610 class meeting about the need to remain sensitive and patient, and a discussion based on change theory the developmental stages in technology adoption and diffusion, were very helpful to me. Subsequently, I became increasingly more intuitive about Gwen's needs. Additionally, this mentoring experience again drove home the value of collaboration. As Chuang put it in Chapter 5 of this book, "being a mentor doesn't mean that I have mastered all the technology skills." Rather, it has afforded me the opportunity to continue to learn through my experience and that of my classmates, about the plethora of issues related to technology in schools. These issues include teacher-related barriers to technology integration, such as having to learn new skills while dealing with already packed schedules, and an awareness of the fact that there is no "one size fits all" approach to technology learning. I cannot overemphasize the importance of just-in-time support for adult technology learning, leadership issues in technology diffusion and curriculum integration, the significance of teacher-to-teacher mentoring, and the pairing of teachers with experience in similar curriculum areas. My knowledge of curriculum development and instructional technology, coupled with my teaching experience and experience in the application of technology, made it easier for me to support and assist Gwen in looking at the *what, when,* and *why* of technology use and its integration into the curriculum.

As a result of my own experiences and the knowledge I gained about Gwen's perceptions of barriers to her technology use, I wondered whether or not the rest of the staff had the same concerns. Consequently, I created a small two-question survey to collect data for comparison using the tool shown in Table 8.1.

The results of question one of the survey are summarized in Table 8.2. Interestingly, the data from this survey are similar to those published in reports on teachers' experiences with technology. In a survey of more than half of the schools in Iowa, the Des Moines Register (Beckman, 2001) reported that teachers indicated the following barriers to using technology:

- Lack of training or staff development (83%)
- Insufficient funding (43%)
- Out-of-date hardware and software (22%)
- Inadequate technical support (10%)

Responses to the second question on the survey suggested that teachers wanted both training and time to work on effective technology integration (see Table 8.3). A majority of them expressed a need for modeling/demonstrations and mentoring. The data indicated that the need for individualized mentoring to meet the teachers at their current level of knowledge and skill development is critical.

Table 8.1. King Academy Teacher Technology Survey

1. What do you see as barriers to using technology in the classroom?

   a) Hardware b) Software c) Other?

   Please list

2. What is one thing that can be done to make it easier for you to use technology?

Table 8.2. Summary of Responses to Question 1

Barriers

- Lack of computers and printers for each teacher (equipment)
- Lack of time to introduce new things
- Lack of ideas or strategies for curriculum integration
- There is no support person who can respond to technology problems efficiently
- More software needs to be available to teachers (grade-level appropriate)
- Classroom management becomes a problem (when you only have one or two students using the computer how can you engage the remaining students?)

Table 8.3. Summary of Responses to Question 2

Responses to the second question on the survey suggested that teachers wanted both training and time to work on effective technology integration (see Table 8.2). A majority of them expressed a need for modeling/demonstrations and mentoring. The data indicated that the need for individualized mentoring to meet the teachers at their current level of knowledge and skill development is critical.

Solutions

- Provide training
- Provide staff development
- Allow time to learn and further explore
- Provide opportunities for modeling/demonstrations/mentoring
- Allow time to collaborate with others
- Provide opportunities to observe other teachers using technology in their classroom

NEW DIRECTION FOR THE FUTURE

Gwen was clear that she had learned a lot about technology during our collaborative experience. Rogers' theory, Social Learning Theory, and the CBAM discussed by Sahin in Chapter 2, all suggest that reinvention is a crucial factor leading the successful adoption of technology in teaching.

Hence, the next steps involved helping Gwen modify and make technology more integral to her curriculum and moving it into the hands of the students. This suggested a continuation of the mentoring experience in order to accommodate her personal technology learning needs as well as those related to curriculum integration. In addition, I saw a need to create study groups or learning communities for early childhood and primary education teachers who are integrating technology and to provide peer mentors to support their learning. Research indicated that if teachers were to successfully incorporate a new and complex resource, such as computer software into their teaching practice, they needed access to other people from whom they could learn. Such mentors were either experts who had already mastered the resource or a community of teacher-learners who pooled their efforts and shared their exploratory findings (Marsh, 2000). At the high school and college levels, students served as mentors to support peers, staff, and teacher education faculty. Demonstrations by teachers who successfully used technology in their classrooms were also useful to provide the observability attribute of instructional technology that speeds up the innovation-decision process according to Rogers' theory described by Sahin in Chapter 2.

CONCLUSIONS

As a graduate student in the Technology in Teacher Education (CI 610) class and a full time teacher, I was in a different situation than most of the other students in the class. Given my work schedule, I needed to do my mentoring with a colleague, rather than an Iowa State University faculty member. Thus, my case illustrates some of the ways that the mentoring program generalizes to a K–12 environment.

In general, my experiences with my colleague, Gwen, were similar to those of the other graduate students in the class. Although they were mentoring faculty members and I was mentoring a colleague, we still structured our experiences in similar ways and experienced similar challenges. My experience suggests that the technology community formed in a university teacher education community can easily and naturally extend to K–12. During the course, I noticed that my graduate student colleagues were especially interested in the K–12 applications developed by Gwen and myself and that some of them shared our work with their faculty mentees. This type of connection between K–12 and higher education is useful for both.

Given my positive experience with Gwen and the results of a survey I administered to my colleagues, I believe that the teacher teaching teachers mentoring model is both needed and appropriate for a K–12 environment. I plan to work to expand my experiences and include more teachers in a mentoring program after my experience with Gwen. Eventually, I also believe that using students from K–12 as mentors for teachers might be a good next step for my school.

REFERENCES

Boeckman, J. (2001, March 20). Funds, training, equipment lag for technology in classroom. *Des Moines Register (IA),* p. E1.

Marsh, M. (2000). Teachers teaching teachers: From sharing information in the hallway to desktop movies on the Internet. *Computer Learning.*

National Association for the Education of Young Children (NAEYC). (1996, September). Position statement: Technology and young children ages three through eight. *Young Children, 51*(6), 11–16.

Plotnick, E. (1999). Information literacy: ERIC Digest of K. L. Spitzer, M. B. Eisenberg, & C. A.Lowe, *Information literacy: Essential skills for the information age.* (ERIC Document Reproduction Service No. 427777).

Smith, S. J. & O'Bannon, B. (1999). Faculty members infusing technology across teacher education: A mentorship model. *Teacher Education and Special Education, 22*(2), 123–135.

Thompson, A. & Schmidt, D. (1994). A three-year program to infuse technology throughout a teacher education program: Year 3 update. In B. Robin, & D. Willis (Eds.), *Technology and Teacher Education Annual 1996* (p. 495–498). Charlottesville, VA: Association for the Advancement of Computing in Education.

CHAPTER 9

MENTOR ME THIS! TECHNOLOGY MENTORING IN A SECONDARY SCHOOL

Jeannette Babcock and Mary Ohaver Moermond

In the fall of 1999, graduate students in the Iowa State University (ISU) mentoring class, as described in Chapter 1, were allowed to choose either an ISU professor or a K–12 staff member as a mentee. Because I worked in a public school at the time, the choice of one of my secondary school colleagues was a perfect option for me. This chapter begins with a narrative of my experience as a mentor along with a segment in the words of my mentee, Mary. The second section of the chapter is a description of the mentoring project that we began with a small group of mentors and mentees the following semester. A brief overview of staff development needs and technology competencies of teachers introduces this section, as an integral part of the staff development proposal.

MENTOR PROFILE

The CI610 mentoring assignment allowed me to combine my roles as a high school library media specialist and as a graduate student pursuing a Ph.D. in Curriculum and Instruction (CI) with an emphasis on educational technology. I had taught staff development classes for our local Area Edu-

Faculty Mentoring: The Power of Students in Developing Technology Expertise, pages 105–119

cational Agency for 11 years, so my interest in this area was especially strong. The mentoring project allowed me to share my commitment to lifelong learning with a colleague, which is an important feature of the mentoring process as Lindstrom points out in Chapter 4.

I had been granted an unpaid, 2/5 time leave for one year, so I worked three days a week as a library media specialist and attended classes on the other two days (and nights).

MENTEE PROFILE

Mary Ohaver Moermond, a Johnston High School French teacher, agreed to work with me for this project. She taught Advanced Placement French over the Iowa Communications Network (ICN), which is a fiber optic network connecting many schools throughout Iowa with real time interactive video and audio. She also participated in local technology staff development, as well as an intensive foreign language institute, so she had a fairly good background in the use of a variety of technologies. However, her primary use of computers, similar to that of the mentees in Chapters 4 and 5, consisted of word processing and e-mail, plus some classroom management for grades and attendance.

Originally, we planned to meet during one of her planning periods each week or for one hour after school. The specific day would likely vary depending on her schedule or mine.

MENTORING IN A 9–12 SETTING: HIGHLIGHTS OF THE SESSIONS

Since we had known each other, both professionally and personally, for about twenty years, the preliminary getting acquainted session was held over the telephone early in the semester. Mary indicated that her goal was to include more technology in her French 1, 3, and 4 classes. Her new textbooks included several Internet activities, so she also wanted help with those. It was interesting to see a publisher's view of infusion of technology into a curriculum.

Another of her goals resulted from her participation in the New Technologies in Foreign Language Institute at Iowa State University. During those eight days, she heard about a Jeopardy-type game that a presenter had created. She bought a copy and hoped to learn how to use the game in her French classes.

My first goal was to help her connect the computer and the 32 inch monitor in her classroom in order for her to present information from the

Figure 9.1. Working in Mary's classroom.

computer to her whole class. With copies of the activities in her teacher's guide and the Jeopardy program, I could then show her how the presentation process worked. However, as mentioned in previous chapters, as well as in class discussions, Mary's goals guided us.

Weeks went by in our attempt to make the Jeopardy game work. Even e-mail messages to the developer and the promise of another diskette didn't solve the problem. So one Friday, Mary and I met in her classroom and developed a list of other options that we could try while we waited for the replacement diskette (see Figure 9.1). The goals she chose were:

1. Find a way to download the worksheets that accompany the French 1 textbook. These worksheets included Internet sites that relate to the French 1 course.
2. Learn to project Internet sites on the monitor in her classroom.
3. Find sites with current French money and the new Euros, since the textbook still had only the older monetary illustrations.
4. Consider other web searches that French 3 and French 4 students might do.

One French 4 lesson included a discussion of Roman and Gothic cathedrals. Some of these attractions actually had web sites relating to them, so finding a list of web addresses was a start. When I asked her to consider challenging her students to do this work, she was a little hesitant.

I suggested that she think of ways that students might demonstrate their new knowledge as a result of web searches (and maybe even book searches). They might create a slide show or simply show a web site and discuss it with the class. She was a little unsure about the value of these activities.

However, before the end of the session, I made sure that we connected the computer and the large screen monitor. Then, with one click of her video distribution remote control, she had the computer screen on the large monitor, with an option to zoom into one of nine areas of the screen

Figure 9.2. With the click of one button!

(see Figure 9.2). She was pleased with the result. She had been teaching in the ICN room for a couple of years and was a little spoiled with the technology available in that room. I think she was pleasantly surprised that she could easily do some of the same things right in her classroom. As Sahin mentions in Chapter 2, simplicity of instructional technology is among the key innovation attributes that leads to the rapid integration of the technology into teaching. Connecting the computer with the large screen monitor in her classroom would simplify classroom technology use for Mary and was a natural first step in minimizing the complexity of the innovation.

The goal of printing the worksheets from the Internet was more difficult to solve. As Lindstrom and Kouadio report in Chapters 4 and 8, hardware problems must be overcome before technology use is effective. Mary and I discovered that her computer was too old to run the Internet browser that was required for downloading the pages, and also that a color printer was needed. We couldn't really fix either of these issues at the time, so I printed a few of the lessons at home to show advantages of using these Internet sources for classroom activities and shared them with her. I knew that relative advantage was another significant factor, like the simplicity attribute, encouraging the use of instructional technology. That way she could decide how important they were.

Our midmorning session did not work very well. Mary thought she shouldn't waste my valuable time in school and didn't want to burden me with coming in on my university class days. I tried to explain that I needed to do it one way or another for my class credit. I also suggested that we might need to spend time during a weekend, if we couldn't find enough time during the week.

SUCCESS

I decided to try one more time with the game diskette, since the promised replacement still hadn't arrived. Mary and I tried to figure out the software together using the trial and error tactics Chuang describes in Chapter 5 and as recommended in class. However, as Li indicates in Chapter 6, sometimes the best tactic is for the mentor to learn the software first. So working on my own, I finally solved the problem and promptly shared the solution with Mary. This seemed to fit our time constraints and her expectations better, without really jeopardizing (pun intended) the mentoring.

Mary and I met in the ICN room (see Figure 9.3), because a newer version of Microsoft Office was loaded on the Power Macintosh there. Using a diskette with the name of the program unchanged, we finally had the right combination and QuizzIt opened (see Figure 9.4).

I briefly showed her some of the features of PowerPoint. When we tried the slide show view, she exclaimed, "That's it," with great relief that we actually found what she expected to be on the diskette. My relief was just as palpable. It had seemed as though we might not reach this goal, especially before my project deadline at the end of the semester. Once we tried all the views, she decided that she preferred the outline view and started to enter vocabulary words. She had created a very nice chart of the whole layout, so this step went quickly. It was obvious that she had spent some time preparing to use this game, so it was especially gratifying to finally see it work.

Figure 9.3. ICN session with Mary.

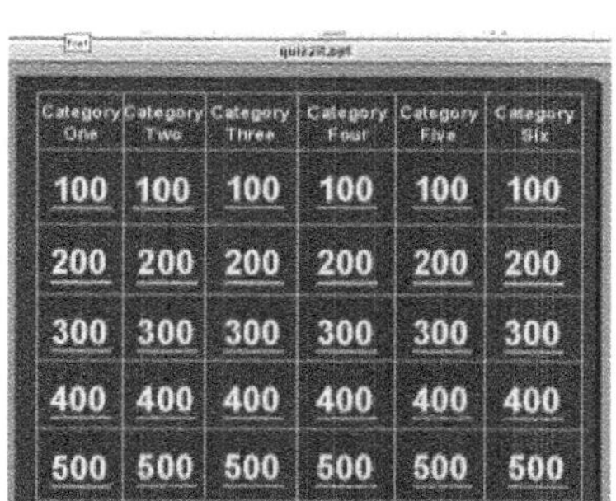

Figure 9.4. The program worked.

Before she entered too many items, I suggested that we check to be sure that the game actually worked correctly. Since I didn't know how it worked, I asked her to show me. She reiterated her favorite phrase, "Remember, I was the dumbest one in the class, so how can I show you?" I replied, "I wasn't there and you at least saw it work, so you know more than I do. Let's try it." Unfortunately, when we clicked on a category in the slide show, gave an answer, checked it, and then returned to the opening window, that category was now blank! We tried several strategies, but the category remained blank.

Luckily, we actually had one file with a class name and the original file. When we opened the original, all the categories were fine. This gave me an opportunity to reiterate the importance of saving the file with a new name for each class and also to show her how the copy and paste commands worked. Since I was not sure what the designer did to the template, I said, "Let's see if this will work. If it doesn't we can just start over again." I hoped that this sense of not being able to ruin anything would encourage her to be more adventuresome in other computer endeavors. In this case, the copy and paste commands brought back all of the vocabulary and translations that she had just entered. At this point, Mary was on her own and quite satisfied. Once again, our experience showed the importance of the trialability attribute in using instructional technology. In our case, I realized that the mentoring program successfully created a one-on-one learning environment with an opportunity for a trial basis for Mary.

When I checked with her a little later, we talked some more about how she might use this program with her class. She said that they had just completed the chapter with these words in them, but I suggested that she might use it as a review or as an introduction to the game. I added that then she could even bring her classes to the ICN room for the games. She replied "I never thought of that. The kids love to come down here, and with two big screens, it should be even better than in my room" (see Figure 9.5). At this point, the technology had just become a tool to assist in thinking outside the box. That could be as important as her increased computer skills.

This activity was exactly what Mary wanted to do, so she made rapid progress. As described in Chapter 2, in Roger's terms, Mary had seen the

Figure 9.5. Mary's class in the ICN room.

relative advantage of using this application and thus was motivated toward learning and adoption. We covered terms, such as the difference between a program like PowerPoint and a file or template such as the Jeopardy game. We discussed the basic operations of PowerPoint and how most commands were similar from one program to another. We talked some more about options for keeping score, since this game didn't seem to have that feature built into it. Then I mentioned the difference between shareware games, such as this one, and more expensive ones that might automatically keep score and also allow random access to the vocabulary words. I told her that I would like to sit in on a game session once she had it ready. She was excited and I was satisfied, but she continued to protest that I was spending too much time helping her. It was nice to be appreciated!

We then turned our attention to the CD-ROM discs that came with her new textbook. In a fashion typical of our experience thus far, the first one didn't work! I took it to another computer to be sure the problem did not lie with the use of her slightly older computer. Even on a Power PC it didn't work. Then with a little mental problem solving, I decided to check the other two CDs in the folder. Sure enough, both of them included the Installer, and lo and behold, both of them worked. I checked in again with Mary and explained the situation. She agreed to take care of requesting a replacement CD from the company. She used the second CD and installed the program on her computer, connected it to the large monitor, and voila—another goal was met. We were getting better!

As the other authors in this book indicate, active participation by the mentees was an important part of the program. Early in the semester, we held an initial session for all mentors and mentees to briefly share their goals. Near the end of the semester, we met for a meal and shared success stories. At one point, the mentees were asked to write their views of the program. Mary's own words indicate that she was as satisfied with this experience as I was.

FROM THE VIEWPOINT OF THE MENTEE

As far as I'm concerned, working with Jeannette Babcock this semester was a very successful endeavor. She spent a lot of time helping me recognize what I already knew and making me feel more and more comfortable about using the computer in the classroom. We worked on computer units to use in class, a computer Jeopardy game, and the CD-ROM programs that accompanied my new French I textbook. The computer Jeopardy game took hours for her to have up and running for me so that I could use it in class with students. Not only did it involve time with me *and* computer time, but she had to correspond extensively with its author to make it compatible with my computer.

Jeannette has been *very* helpful in suggesting new computer projects to be incorporated into my curriculum. The Gothic and Roman architecture unit in French IV was a good example. She thought it would be a good idea for each student to take a different cathedral or church, do a web search on it, and then present the findings to the class. The students used a computer connected to the large television in the classroom for their presentations, so that the whole class could benefit. The students really enjoyed the unit. Both they and I learned a lot more about the architecture of that time period *and* it took very little outside preparation on my part.

Fortunately for me, Jeannette's schedule is very compatible with mine, so I know we'll spend a lot more time together, adding technology to my curriculum. She's been extremely easy to work with and more important, she's been very patient with this computer rookie.

SUMMARY

Two examples illustrated Mary's confidence and her technology growth. First, she was able to fix an audio problem with the CD and the large monitor with only verbal directions from me. Later, she decided to use the CD in the ICN room and installed the program on that computer, again without help—in fact without even needing verbal directions. Her own words, "Look, no mentor needed," sum up our experience (see Figure 9.6).

Between the readings and discussions in class and the mentoring process itself, I was able to report to the class that the experience worked as well at the high school level as it did at other levels. The stories of other students in the class and those who participated in the writing of this book were all quite similar even though the mentees ranged from elementary teachers to university faculty. The phrase "no mentor needed" and others

Figure 9.6. No mentor needed.

very similar to it resounded in descriptions of the mentoring process. Mary's new found independence in using the technology with "no mentor needed" suggested that she had reached the stage in her adoption where she could work by herself to adapt or reinvent (or reproduce in Social Learning Theory and refocus in the Concerns-Based Adoption Model) the technology for her own purposes. Throughout the stories in this book, this phenomenon of arriving at independent use of the technology provides evidence of the effectiveness of one-on-one mentoring in helping mentees move to higher levels of innovation adoption.

Mary and I enjoyed the mutual benefits of mentoring similar to those Li, Chuang, and Kouadio describe. Besides enjoying the collegial learning that is directly related to mentoring, we also became better problem-solvers in regard to equipment and software, as well as classroom activities and projects. From our experience, we better understood that collegial collaboration and interaction, described as interpersonal communication channels by Sahin in Chapter 2, were key in the success of the mentoring program in making the use of instructional technologies institutionalized. Collaboration between teachers and media specialists is sometimes illusive, so this experience was especially beneficial to me. The result of our collaboration was a step toward infusion of technology in one classroom. As Darling-Hammond (1992) says, the process was as important as the content.

This one-on-one mentoring experience was so powerful that it became a part of technology staff development in our high school and continues to be the research focus in my doctoral program. The details of the pilot project and the first year of the program make up the remainder of this chapter. Moving from Mary's story to our school-wide mentoring efforts, the story now goes from Mary's individual adoption process to a more general process designed to encourage the diffusion of technology integration throughout Johnston High School.

THE JOHNSTON HIGH SCHOOL EXPERIENCE

Based on reviews of the literature, class discussions, and my personal experience with the one-on-one mentoring assignment, I proposed, to the Johnston High School (JHS) Technology Team, that we try this staff development model. School district teams were in the process of developing technology standards and benchmarks for students and a rubric of technology competencies for teachers based on recognized models (Bray, 1999; ISTE, 2000). These standards, benchmarks, and competencies influenced the decision of the JHS Technology Team to use the mentoring model of staff development, especially since it also matched the features of an effective staff development program as described in the literature and in Chapter 3. Highlights of the literature and my professional experience, as related to public schools, are included in the next section.

Over the years, schools across the country tried several models of staff development designed to increase the use of technology by teachers and students. The most common model focused on hardware and software training led by an outside or local expert during inservice or released time. Unfortunately, this staff development model has had little impact on the use of technology in classrooms (Atkins & Vasu, 1998; McKenzie, 1991; Scrogan, 1989; Topper, 2000). Workshops, conferences, and college courses increased the technology knowledge and skills of individuals or small groups. Area Education Agencies (AEAs) and vendors offered a train-the-trainer model of staff development designed especially for local experts. Longer sessions with more collaboration followed in another attempt to increase classroom use of computers (Apple, 1995), but exemplary models and technology infusion were still not common (Honey, Millan Culp, & Carrigg, 1999; Richardson, 2000; Willis, Thompson, & Sadera, 1999).

Technology staff development models that focus on specific and varied needs of teachers are more effective than "one-size-fits-all" sessions. Using local and national standards, competency lists, and surveys as the basis for technology staff development is one way to tailor the sessions (Brearton & Shuttleworth, 1999; Vojtek & O'Brien Vojtek, 1999; Zehr, 1999). Flexible times, recognition or remuneration, support, hands-on activities, and collaborative learning are important to busy teachers (Goldman, Cole, & Syer 1999; Richardson, 2000; Topper, 2000). The one-on-one mentoring model addresses many of these needs and concerns.

JOHNSTON HIGH SCHOOL PILOT STUDY

Several teachers applied to be mentors or mentees and we chose seven mentors. Two district technology people assisted in the selection of the mentors and mentees. With nine mentees selected, we had an opportunity to study various combinations: one-on-one, one-on-two, and two-on-three, based on the goals of the mentees and the expertise of the mentors.

We struggled with the details of the program the first semester. We spent some time determining requirements and the direction that the group would take. A district technology staff person worked with us and offered excellent suggestions. The mentors helped each other considerably. For the first semester, that mutual assistance illustrated a major strength of the program. The mentors attempted to meet every other week for about 45 minutes to encourage each other, share new technology developments, and

Figure 9.7. Mentor meeting.

Figure 9.8. Mentor and mentee.

report on their mentoring progress. A meeting of part of the group is shown in Figure 9.7. With a larger group, the mentor who selected and shared the topic for the session usually used a video projector for the presentation.

At first it seemed as if the mentors struggled with the hardware. They were given PowerBooks to use in their classrooms, and as their personal computers, which allowed them to take the computer with them for mentee sessions, if necessary. The portability also enabled the mentors to put in a lot of their own time increasing their own technology skills. As an added incentive, the mentors could earn their Power Books in lieu of pay, by logging a certain number of hours in the program for three years.

Once the mentors and mentees were working as collaborative teams, the next step involved setting goals, based on the needs and competency levels of the mentees, as indicated by the district technology rubric. The mentors were expected to meet with their mentees about an hour every other week during the school year (see Figure 9.8). Between those sessions, the mentors could increase their own technology skills independently, share expertise with other mentors, take AEA staff development classes alone or with a mentee, and/or ask for assistance from the two leaders. Mentors were also encouraged to use some excellent programs from the Internet on their own, with their mentee, or with other mentors. Again, this allowed them to structure their staff development time to meet busy schedules.

The mentoring model of technology staff development addressed the teacher needs and the staff development needs mentioned above and elsewhere in this book. Our pilot project gave us an opportunity to see how well it worked and the group was very positive about wanting to see the program continue.

A FULL YEAR OF TECHNOLOGY MENTORING

Following the one-semester pilot study, this program was expanded to 10 mentors and 11 mentees for the following school year. Although the mentors were enthusiastic about the program, there were some ups and downs. District technology staff members were concerned about accountability, since the Power Books (equipment-in-lieu of pay) involved funds from the staff development budget. In addition, they wanted to be sure that the mentors and mentees addressed more than software skill development. In response to these concerns, the mentors agreed to encourage their mentees to formulate two goals. One goal would focus on a technology skill that the mentee wanted to improve personally. The other would focus on a curriculum modification to expand the use of technology by students.

Even though these two categories of goals were to be used as guidelines, one mentee had another agenda, namely finding a way to add more equipment to his department. As a group, the mentors, and even the administrators, were unsure how to help that mentor and mentee bring their goals more in line with the expectations. This dilemma resolved itself when the mentee teacher moved the following year. However, it forced us to try to write future expectations even more clearly.

The mentors spent approximately half of the recommended staff development time working with their mentees. They divided the other half evenly between personal learning, to increase their own technology competencies, and supporting each other either formally during meetings or informally at other times.

During the selection process for the first set of mentors, we quickly realized that we needed written criteria to help make the next selection process more accurate. We developed a rubric based on the mentor application. It improved both the quality of the applications and the ease of the selection process. We also used the staff technology skill rubric adopted by the school district as another part of the selection process for both mentors and mentees.

As with all projects, there were some challenges. Some of the mentors contributed the recommended number of hours, but others were unable to do so. Schedule conflicts were often a problem, even though each pair was allowed to pick the time and place for the mentoring sessions. The logistics of the personal ownership of the Power Books concerned us all year. Although we read examples of equipment used in lieu of pay, we never quite determined the details of a contract that spelled out the responsibilities of the mentors and of the district. One district staff member recommended a five-year depreciation cycle, but stopped short of creating a contract. Incentives for the mentees were not finalized. At one time we talked about the possibility of purchasing one iBook for the mentees to share and then awarding it in some way to one of them at the end of the year. Due to budget constraints, this was not done and one mentee was a little upset. She continued as a mentee the next year, but it might have dampened the enthusiasm of other potential mentees.

Accountability for staff development time and resources was a concern of the administrators, but changes in the expectations for the second year seemed to satisfactorily address that issue. Each succeeding year after their first year, mentors would be expected to spend somewhat less time on their own learning and more on the mentoring process. Third-year mentors were also expected to share their expertise with larger groups, such as departments, cluster groups with similar interests or needs, or even the full staff. All of the mentors agreed to these increased expectations.

The excitement, professional conversations, collaboration, and feelings of accomplishment exhibited in the first few months of this project indicated that this was a very successful and effective method of staff development. All of the mentors, except one who already owned a Power Book, continued the program into the second year. Other staff members asked when they could become mentors or mentees. This plan used the elements of staff development recommended by researchers as likely to be most effective, and it seemed to be working. As it evolves from year to year, we hope to keep the best of one-on-one mentoring and modify it to meet our local needs. We will also continue with other staff development models and strategies, so that the needs of staff members are met in a variety of settings using methods that meet their personal and professional needs.

CONCLUSION

In this chapter, I described the extension of the ISU faculty mentoring program to the world of the secondary school. Although most of the elements of the faculty mentoring program generalized to the high school situation, the mentors for the high school teachers were peers rather than graduate students. In one case, I was the mentor for a French teacher and when this experience proved successful, I established a teacher mentoring program at the school. In this teacher mentoring program, I used technology experienced teachers as mentors for their less experienced peers.

The words of the mentors and mentees sum up their experiences in this high school teacher mentoring program. One mentor stated, "I am confi-

Figure 9.9. Mentor helping mentor.

dent that this program is going to be an excellent learning opportunity for me as I work with the other mentors" (see Figure 9.9).

One mentee said, "I felt somewhat intimidated when I had to tell [my mentor] some of the things that I didn't know how to do." At first glance that sounded a little negative, but it also revealed a level of trust that was not likely to be found in a larger group setting. Both mentors and mentees overwhelmingly approved of this staff development process and wanted to see it continue.

Additional comments from several mentors and mentee are included in Table 9.1. Names have been replaced with generic terms.

Table 9.1. Comments from Mentors and Mentees

Excitement	*Learning*
• Wow! [When something was shared between mentors and it worked]. • The excitement of the two mentees in learning new uses for the video distribution system and the computer to TV connection is gratifying for me. • I am excited with [my mentee's] enthusiasm to use technology in his science classes. • I enjoyed the [mentee's] excitement.	• This graphing calculator is awesome. [Mentor learning along with mentee] • I am always surprised at how much I learn in various situations. • I learned so much and spent about 5 hours a week since February [to May] of my own time working on what I learned.
Impact on students	*Strength of the program*
• Student presentations were well done and met the expectations of the instructor [mentee as reported to the mentor]. • My goals were discussed and modified so they would meet student goals as well. • Opened up new plans for speeches. • Wealth of new material.	• It allows effective communication, one-on-one questions and answers. • I was able to bounce around ideas, then try one! Mentor was exceptional. • Teacher centered. • I enjoy the coaching approach. • Having mentor and mentee close by each other was a strength of the program.

REFERENCES

Apple, Inc. (1995). *Apple education research reports: A collection that highlights the role of technology in teaching and learning.* Eugene, OR: International Society for Technology in Education.

Atkins, N. E., & Vasu, E. S. (1998, May). The teaching with technology instrument: Effectively measuring where teachers are and planning for staff development. *Learning & Leading with Technology, 25*(8), 35–39.

Bray, B. (1999, January). Heartland AEA Technology Leadership Institute. Des Moines, IA

Brearton, M. S., & Shuttleworth, S. (1999, Winter). Racing a comet. *Journal of Staff Development, 20*(1), 30–33.

Darling-Hammond, L. (1992). Building learner-centered schools: Developing professional capacity, policy, and political consensus. One of three papers in *Building learner-centered schools: Three perspectives.* New York: Columbia University.

Goldman, S., Cole, K., & Syer, C. (1999). *The technology/content dilemma.* Paper presented at The Secretary's Conference on Educational Technology. Retrieved March 31, 2000 from http://www.ed.gov/Technology/TechConf/1999/whitepapers/paper4.html.

Honey, M., McMillan Culp, K., & Carrigg, F. (1999). *Perspectives on technology and education research: Lessons from the past and present.* Paper presented at The Secretary's Conference on Educational Technology. Retrieved March 31, 2000 from http://www.ed.gov/Technology/TechConf/1999/whitepapers/paper1.html#2.

International Society for Technology in Education (ISTE). (2000, April). Technology standards. *ISTE Update, 12*(7), 1–2.

McKenzie, J. (1991, April). Designing staff development for the information age. *From Now On: The Educational Technology Journal, 1*(4). Retrieved April 6, 2000, from http://staffdevelop.org/sd1.html.

Richardson, J. (2000, Winter). Learning benefits everyone: Award winning schools point to the best in professional development. [Electronic version]. *Journal of Staff Development, 21*(1), 54–59.

Scrogan, L. (1989, January). The OTA report: Teachers, training, and technology. *Classroom Computer Learning, 9*(4), 80–85.

Topper, A. (2000, April). *Professional growth: Theoretical rationale.* Retrieved April 6, 2000, from Michigan State University, College of Education Web site: http://commtechlab.msu.edu/sites/letsnet/frames/bigideas/b9/b9theor.html.

Vojtek, B. & Vojtek, R. O. (1999, Winter). Flung into motion. *Journal of Staff Development, 20*(1), 67–69.

Willis, J., Thompson, A., & Sadera, W. (1999). Research on technology and teacher education: Current status and future directions. *Educational Technology Research and Development, 47*(4), 29–45.

Zehr, M. A. (1999, September 23). Moving teachers along a competency continuum. *Education Week, Special Report: Technology Counts '99,* 37–38.

CHAPTER 10

LEARING TO MENTOR

A Student's Perspective

Natalie Johnson

Using a technology learning model suggested by Chisholm (1994), this chapter presents and analyzes a one-on-one mentoring case. The chapter begins with background on technology mentoring, followed by an exploration of the mentoring process including the challenges, triumphs, and outcomes. Throughout the chapter, there is an emphasis on connecting the mentoring experiences to the literature on mentoring and technology learning. The chapter concludes with suggested creative strategies and tips for approaching the mentoring process.

INTRODUCTION

The idea of students teaching teachers about technology is certainly not a new one. Trotter (1999) describes today's college students as having a "natural affinity for technology" (p. 45). There are instances where students can be asked to help their instructors develop skills in using technology. Chisholm (1994) gives a classical example of how students can be used as teaching resources in helping instructors and other students develop technology skills.

Faculty Mentoring: The Power of Students in Developing Technology Expertise, pages 121–133

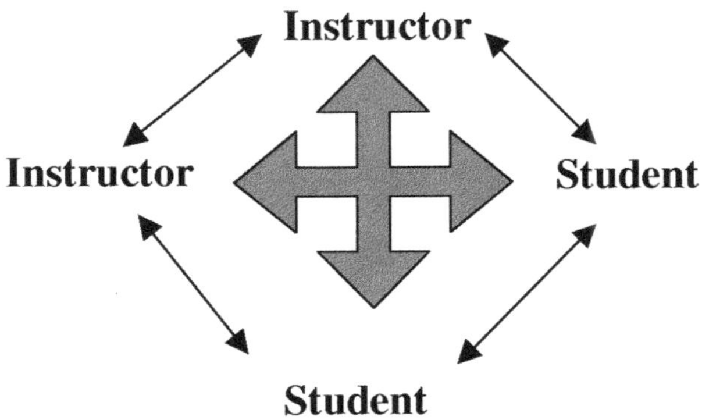

Figure 10.1. Multidimensional teaching and learning web (adapted from Chisholm, 1994).

A multidirectional technology learning paradigm is postulated by Chisholm, where administrators learn from instructors, instructors learn from each other, instructors learn from students, students learn from instructors, and students learn from each other. In this regard, teaching and learning become reciprocal and multidimensional as shown in Figure 10.1.

Using this multidirectional reciprocal model, I will navigate readers through my experiences with the faculty technology mentoring program as part of the requirement for the Curriculum and Instruction course CI610 at Iowa State University (ISU). As indicated in Chapter 1, this program has been beneficial to both instructors and students for over a decade.

In the ISU faculty technology mentoring program, all four dimensions of Chisholm's multidirectional teaching and learning web are evident. However, the student-mentoring instructor is the strongest link. There is also a degree of reciprocal mentoring because, to a lesser degree, instructors mentor students, as Chuang emphasizes in Chapter 5. In addition, students mentor students informally because of the supportive network that is created in the class. Almost all the stories in this book emphasize the importance of this supportive network for the mentors. Each week there was a debriefing session whereby students spoke of their triumphs and challenges. It was not uncommon for students having challenges with a concept or technology issue to communicate with peers to get needed help. In fact, one student suggested that another student in the class mentored her constantly. In addition, there were times when a student invited his/her colleague to work with the mentee. Instructors also received help from each other in dealing with various technology issues in this multidimensional mentoring model.

Faculty members interested in the mentoring program indicate their willingness to participate to the CI610 instructor. Generally, students are matched with a mentee based on the student's area(s) of expertise, strengths, and interests, as well as the interests and needs of the mentee. As Sahin mentions in Chapter 2, this matching is very crucial for the success of the program and helps the mentors easily show the mentees the relative advantage and compatibility of instructional technologies with their needs and interests. Student mentees did not always have the specific software expertise desired by the mentee, however, and there were situations where students as mentors had to learn how to use the software and/or the technological application that matched the mentee's interest. As detailed in several stories in this book, it was not uncommon for both mentor and mentee to learn technology applications during the mentoring process.

The case described in this chapter is the continuing story of technology adoption of a senior professor. While the first story involving this professor focused upon his initial adoption of technology, this chapter describes his developing journey into more complex technology use.

MENTEE PROFILE

Dr. Abelson was a regular participant in the faculty-mentoring program. His experiences that centered on learning PowerPoint with his mentor Denise are documented in Chapter 4 of this book. Dr. Abelson has been a professor of special education at ISU for the past 24 years in the Department of Curriculum and Instruction. His class, Special Education 250, is a prerequisite for several other courses in the teacher education program and it also satisfies one of the diversity requirements for majors across the university. As a result, he has a class of over 250 students each semester. This class is held in a large lecture hall that is technology friendly. Therefore, access to technology was not an obstacle for my mentee.

In studies carried out by Leggett & Persichitte (1998) and Moskal, Martin, and Foshee (1997), three major obstacles to technology integration were identified: (1) lack of required equipment in the classroom, (2) lack of time to learn how to use technology, and (3) lack of funds. Other factors cited in the literature include pedagogical issues, organizational issues related to incentives and rewards, change in practice, and expertise (Beaudoin, 1990; Dillon & Walsh, 1992; Schrum, 1995). In addition, the literature suggests that personal characteristics of teachers/instructors, workloads, technical and administrative problems, and fear of reduced student interaction are barriers for technology integration. In this mentoring project, many of these challenges were not issues for my mentee. First, the classroom where Dr. Abelson had his class was equipped with all the technology "bells and whistles" including an Internet connection. Secondly, the issue of time to learn how to use technology was negotiated from the first meeting. We were aware of the requirements for meeting at least one hour per week. We designed our schedules accordingly and kept our weekly appointments. Finally, the areas of funding, pedagogy, and organizational issues were not barriers to learning and integrating technology in Dr. Abelson's class. Learning how to integrate technology at a comfortable pace, in a non-threatening environment, with one's own equipment can shift to embrace technology worthwhile (Carr, 1999). Using Rogers' (2003) model, these characteristics emphasized by Carr relate to the simplicity (the opposite of complexity) attribute of an innovation. Having already participated in the mentoring program during previous semesters, Dr. Abelson had had experiences emphasizing the simplicity of the innovation and had integrated technology into his classes enthusiastically.

Dr. Abelson infused technology in his class through the use of PowerPoint presentations and blackboard.com as the managing software for his classes. The infusion of technology in the educational process presented new ways for Dr. Abelson to enliven and enrich his teaching/learning strategy. Dr. Abelson moved up the ladder of technology integration in his classes. This was in keeping with several research findings.

A number of researchers (Cuban, 1993; Evans-Andris, 1995; Duhaney, 1999; Zimmerman, 2001) investigated teachers' reactions to the use of technology in their classrooms over time. Table 10.1 gives a comparison of how different groups of teachers viewed and responded to this change in technology usage. Between 1993 and 2001 different groups of teachers responded to technology usage in a similar fashion from fear and avoidance to optimism and experimentation.

Table 10.1. Teachers' Initial and Subsequent Reactions to Technology Usage

Group	*Cuban (1993)*	*Evans-Andris (1995)*	*Duhaney (1999)*	*Zimmerman (2001)*
Group 1	Intimidated (technophiles)	Avoidance	Some with fear	Mighty resisters
Group 2	Receptive (preservationists)	Integration	Sporadically	Needing encouragement and support
Group 3	Optimists	Technology specialists	Risk takers	Risk-taking, experimenters, pioneers and champions

In my view, my mentee was operating in Group 2. According to Franklin, Turner, Kariuki and Duran (2001), Dr. Abelson was operating at the intermediate level. Dr. Abelson was very receptive to learning how to improve his technology skills, specifically PowerPoint presentations and blackboard.com capabilities. Based on my experience during fall 2001, working closely with Dr. Abelson led me to the conclusion that he was willing to continue developing the technology skills and competences required for him to advance to the third stage of becoming an active and confident experimenter. Dr. Abelson's goals for the semester were in keeping with the further development of his technology skills:

- Becoming more adept with PowerPoint.
- Learning how to create links in Blackboard.com.
- Identifying and using as many capabilities of Blackboard.com as possible.
- Applying for a technology grant.
- Searching for relevant cases and software addressing special education that could be integrated into class lectures.

As an important element of Social Learning Theory (Rogers, 2003), goal setting was the pivotal point of our first mentor/mentee contact. For a mentoring relationship to be worthwhile, it is important to agree on learning goals or outcomes in a collaborative manner. According to Van Ast (2000), the essence of mentoring is the individual relationship and mutual goal setting between mentor and mentee. Although the mentor may choose a variety of strategies and activities to help the mentee grow and develop professional competence, attitudes and behaviors, "it is the qualitative nature of the relationship, which will ultimately determine success" (p. 6) in achieving the outlined goals.

MENTOR PROFILE

I am a sociable, practical, and intense individual who thrives on challenges. I am from the country of Jamaica where I was trained as a high school teacher. Currently, I am a Ph.D. candidate in both Educational Leadership and Policy Studies (ELPS) and Curriculum and Instructional Technology (CIT) at Iowa State University.

Since coming to ISU in 1998, my interest and skills in technology integration, leadership, and change have matured. Prior to taking technology courses in the Curriculum and Instruction department, I had no experience with technology integration. However, I was always curious and I had a positive attitude towards technology usage.

Understanding the pedagogical usage of technology in teacher education is of importance to me. As a result, it was very appealing to me when I learned that there was a mentoring (practical application) aspect to the course. Initially, the concept of mentoring a professor made me anxious, nervous, and fearful. How could I, a student, mentor a professor in technology usage? Could I choose an instructor with whom I am comfortable to mentor? Would I be able to succeed in this activity? These were some of the questions I wrestled with in the first few weeks of class. I was able to overcome my anxiety when I learned that two of us in the class would be mentoring Dr. Abelson. I had great confidence in the technological capability of my colleague. Such a partnership and team worked effectively for all three of us.

As the mentoring experience progressed, I developed personal goals for my mentee that were driven by the goals of my mentee. My goals spanned the four constructs postulated by Van Ast (2000):

1. *Competence.* Mastery of knowledge, skills, and applications in Blackboard.com.
2. *Self-confidence.* Strong belief in his capability of making good decisions regarding technology integration in his course.
3. *Self-direction.* The assurance and ability of my mentee to take charge of using a variety of technology in his class based on the needs of and usefulness to student learning.
4. *Professionalism.* To continue using technology to enhance his pedagogy and professionalism in the field of special education.

I was committed to the task of helping my mentee fulfill these goals. I felt I was entrusted with the "sacred" responsibility of helping my mentee achieve his goals and grow. This was in a similar manner in which Odysseus, the King of Ithaca entrusted his friend (mentor) with the care of his son as he went to fight the Trojan War—according to the mentoring legend[1] (Carr, 1999).

THE MENTORING PROCESS

At the start of the mentoring process, Dr. Abelson had two of us as student mentors. In the first half of the semester we accomplished the first three goals. As a team, my colleague and I worked with Dr. Abelson in all areas of his needs and/or challenges. The literature on mentoring highlights challenges that may surface in mentoring relationships. Warring and Lindquist (1989) found that the lack of clear goals for mentors and mentees could lead to potential challenges including poor communication, which in turn hinders progress. Another challenge that can be disruptive results when the mentee is not as participatory in the teaching/learning activities for the mentee to develop the skills deemed necessary. This can lead to the mentee becoming dependent on the mentor (King, 1991).

---

1. The roots of mentoring can be traced back to more than 5000 years to Africa, where guides were provided to show young people "the way" (Carr, 1999).

In my mentor relationship with Dr. Abelson, the above-mentioned challenges did not characterize our relationship. However, two other challenges surfaced during the semester as we worked together. They were technological and personal challenges.

Technological Challenges

Challenge #1: It is ironic that I was chosen as the mentor and I became challenged with "simple" technological procedures. The first technological challenge we experienced as a team was uploading a file to Blackboard.com that would make it easier for Dr. Abelson's students to post their plans for their group project. My colleague, Dr. Abelson, and I tried all the options we knew to upload the table to Blackboard.com, but none of the options were successful. This was frustrating for all three of us. We encouraged each other, and eventually we resorted to sending the document to students via e-mail rather than as a link on Blackboard.com.

Challenge #2: A second technological challenge was the loss of a file with over 100 PowerPoint slides. "This was it," I thought. Dr. Abelson was distraught, angry, and frustrated. We tried all the trouble shooting options that we knew without success. So, we asked two computer technicians to help us retrieve the document. When Dr. Abelson realized that the computer technicians went through the same trouble shooting procedures we had already explored with no success, he was extremely discouraged. A look of disbelief, discouragement, and disappointment all intermingled on my mentee's face as he pounded the desk with his fist.

In my opinion, if my mentee did not see the value of integrating technology in the classroom, that refers to Rogers' (2003) relative advantage attribute of innovations, he would have given up due to frustration with technology. At this point, the complexity of the innovation was overwhelming to my mentee. I gave my mentee the support and opportunity to vent his frustration. At the same time, I encouraged him not to give up. I offered to help with the entire process of compiling the slides again, but he saw it as "a waste of my time." He then asked for the meeting to be adjourned.

The meeting was aborted, because my mentee was filled with the disappointment of losing an entire semester of hard work. I assured him before I left that I was willing and ready to work with him to get his document together again. I reminded him to save all his work in multiple places to safeguard against losing files in the future.

In retrospect, technology is a useful tool in helping individuals to organize, conduct, and retrieve work with ease and speed. However, technology has a dark side. It is fallible and can fail. Together, my mentee and I learned from this painful experience. This is in keeping with Zachary's (2000) views that mentors and mentees must focus on learning. This learning process starts with self-learning, without which the potential for effectiveness in the learning relationship is greatly reduced and so is the ability to empathize.

Having lost all my computer files to a virus a few weeks earlier, I could understand the frustrations and disappointment my mentee felt. He blamed himself a lot, but I encouraged him by reminding him that it is so easy to lose a file—even when you are a mentor. He was able to smile about that comment, and he definitely felt a little better about himself. Based on this experience the nature of mentoring work was reinforced to me. Zachary (2000) describes the nature of mentoring as follows:

- Mentoring is a powerful growth experience.
- Mentoring is a process of engagement.
- Facilitating effective mentoring begins with self-learning.
- Mentoring with staying power focuses on the learners, the learning process, and learning.

Challenge #3: The third technological challenge occurred close to the end of the semester. Several students in Dr. Abelson's class e-mailed him because they were unable to log into Blackboard.com. My mentee logged on with ease. As a result, he suggested to students that the problem might be with their computers.

At our subsequent meeting we explored the issue. Students were getting anxious about not being able to get in Blackboard.com to do the required readings for their class. Together Dr. Abelson and I visited the Blackboard.com website and found that the mainframe page and the links for students in Special Education 250 to log on had been changed. During our meeting, we called the computer technicians at Blackboard.com and we found a way to work around the changes.

As a result, my mentee and I were armed with the solution to our third technological challenge. Dr. Abelson e-mailed the solution to all the students so they would know how to access the course on Blackboard.com. My mentee asked me to accompany him to his class the following day to give a live demonstration of logging on using the new frame. This went well and some students were asked to participate in the activity of logging on to Blackboard.com during the class. This experience in class created a positive outcome for our struggles with Blackboard.com. This experience supported Rogers' observability and trialability attributes of innovations that both faculty and students should have the opportunity to observe how new technologies can be used and to experience these technologies on a trial base.

Coupled with the technological challenges described, I had a few personal challenges during the mentor/mentee relationship. The following is a description and interpretation of these challenges.

Personal Challenges

This was my first experience with mentoring a professor in using technology. I revised several of my *teaching* strategies in order for the mentor/mentee relationship with Dr. Abelson to be a success. I worked to make these challenges invisible to Dr. Abelson and to deal with them professionally.

First, I had to learn to be the guide on the side, the cheerleader, supporting and encouraging my mentee. Reflection on the mentoring activities brought to the forefront the fact that my initial mentoring style was my high school teaching style/paradigm. In this paradigm, I operated at "giving instruction" more than facilitating, coaching, and being the guide on the side, not the "sage on the stage."

This was a mistake I was glad I caught early in the mentoring relationship. I was able to adjust my style to becoming more student-focused (mentee-focused). In this way, my skills as a mentor were further developed and expanded. For example, I remember in one of our meetings that I wanted so badly to control the mouse as Dr. Abelson and I worked on how to put transitions in the PowerPoint slides. However, my mentee did not give me a chance. Upon reflection on this experience I concluded that this was a very good response from my mentee. Who would benefit most from controlling the mouse? What were my goals and objectives within the mentoring process? What are the goals of my mentee in this process? Who should the focus be placed on, the mentor or the mentee?

I learned from my mistake of wanting to get my hands on the mouse. Instead, I had to give clear instructions at a comfortable pace for my mentee to follow rather than demonstrating or showing him what to do. Simultaneously, my mentee learned how to use the tools in carrying out the processes that I explained to him. After all, the goal of the mentoring experience is for instructors to learn how to use the technology tools efficiently themselves and to advance through the implementation and confirmation stages of the adoption process.

My mentee had an opportunity to ask questions and seek clarifications. Instead of telling Dr. Abelson the answers, I changed my strategy to probing and encouraging him to "toy" with the functions he was curious about because the trialability attribute of an innovation increases the likelihood of the adoption of the innovation, as stated by Sahin in Chapter 2. For example, we discovered how to use the pointer during a slide show in PowerPoint. Dr. Abelson asked, "What will happen if I selected the pen option instead?" My response was, "Go ahead and try it, play with the features and let us see the result." When he selected the pen he realized that he had to carry out two additional steps in getting the pointer to work. So he smiled and said, "It is easier to select the pointer." He tried the action all by himself and he was very excited when he succeeded in getting the pointer to work all by himself. This was another (aha!) learning moment for both Dr. Abelson and myself. When he asked, "How do I get rid of the marks on the slide?" I asked, "What if you click off the slide mode, what would happen?" He clicked from the slide mode and he exclaimed, "YES!" He was really excited to learn how to use the pointer efficiently.

Another personal challenge I faced was the pace at which I wanted to go. I approached this exercise being task-oriented. With my task-oriented approach, I felt a little impatient at times when I did not accomplish the list of activities that I had planned. I had to learn to step back and allow my mentee to be in the driver's seat. Ebbs and flows in the pace at which we accomplished tasks characterized our mentoring process. The ebbs and flow in my mentoring experience with Dr. Abelson served to enrich this learning experience.

I struggled to be creative in the mentee mentor relationship, because I mastered the skills of designing PowerPoint presentations. Having to journal my activities each week gave me the great opportunity to engage in reflective practice (Schön, 1997). This reflection led to meta-cognition in understanding the mentoring process, which, in turn, helped me to understand my role as a mentor. I finally recognized that my role was not to create challenges that I wanted for myself. Rather, my role was to work with Dr. Abelson and help him overcome his challenges with technology integration. According to Wickman (1996), mentors should be frequently reminded of their purpose in the mentoring process, so that the needs of the mentee are always in the forefront.

As we progressed throughout the semester with the mentoring activity, I learned to learn. I was constantly reminded that the role of the mentor is to facilitate learning in a manner in which the knowledge, skills, and competencies that I bring connect with the instructions I give and the actions and ability of my mentee (Zachary, 2000).

WHAT HAVE I LEARNED ABOUT THE MENTORING: WHAT WOULD I DO DIFFERENTLY?

This mentor/mentee activity was a real learning experience for me. Learning in this context is defined as deliberate activities that increase the capacity and willingness of individuals or groups to acquire and apply new knowledge and skills. This leads to growth and maturity to adapt successfully to changes and challenges. Such learning not only empowers individuals to make wise choices but also to solve problems and break new ground.

Such a definition focuses on the individuals making the deliberate efforts to acquire and utilize the knowledge and skills in practical ways. As a result of my learning experience, from this mentoring activity, my understanding and conceptualization of working as a mentee was vastly improved, resulting in a cumulative wealth of knowledge from this experiential learning activity. Conversely, I would like to highlight some limitations I encountered that could be addressed to enrich the mentor/mentee relationships of subsequent students in the future:

- The mentoring literature should be addressed in the experience. Some authors postulate that mentoring is a natural process but my experience dictates otherwise. If I had more background knowledge from the literature I could have been a more effective mentor.
- Grounding students in the mentoring theory can be beneficial. It is vital at the outset to have students develop a clear understanding of the stages of the mentoring process (Krupp, 1997), which can serve a guide to them:
    (1) Initiation stage—relationships are established
    (2) Mentoring stage—the mentor fosters the growth of the mentee
    (3) Termination stage—where independence is encouraged at the appropriate moment
- Help student mentors realize that they need to be relational. I was task-oriented so I lost out on the opportunity to build a sustained social relationship with my mentee.
- Mentors need to understand there is much to be learned from their mentees. I learned classroom management skills from attending classes with my mentee. However, I did not take the opportunity for Dr. Abelson to teach me how to use the features of Blackboard.com, which he was proficient in using. I learned the features on my own. Such an opportunity for my mentee to teach me about technology would have encouraged him to realize that he was an expert in this area.

CONCLUSION

My case involved "second level" mentoring in that I worked with a faculty member who had participated in the program previously. In one sense, my mentee entered the relationship with more experience with mentoring than I. Throughout the experience, I continued to learn how to mentor and to improve my mentoring skills. As I worked with my mentee, I used some of the literature on mentoring and mentoring models to help inform the experience, and I suggest that others use this work as they initiate faculty and/or teacher mentoring programs. I also found the multidirectional technology learning paradigm (Chisholm, 1994) useful in describing and understanding the reciprocal learning that occurred during my mentoring experience and many of the experiences described in this book.

REFERENCES

Beaudoin, M. (1990). The instructor's changing role in distant education. *The American Journal of Distant Education, 4*(2), 21–29.

Carr, R. (1999). *Achieving the future: The role of mentoring in the new millennium.* Paper prepared for the program for the support of women's leadership and representation (PROLEAD). British Columbia, Canada.

Chisholm, I. (1994). Culture and technology: Implications for multicultural teacher education. *Journal of Information Technology for Teacher Education, 3*(2), 218–226.

Cuban, L. (1993). Computers meet classrooms: Classrooms wins. *Teacher's college Record, 95*(2), 185–210.

Dillon, C., & Walsh, S. (1992). Faculty: The neglected resource in distant education. *The American Journal of Distant Education, 6*(3), 5–21.

Duhaney, D. (1999). Technology and the educational process: Transforming classroom activities. *International Journal of Instructional Media, 26*(2), 67–70.

Evans-Andris, M. (1995). Barrier to computer integration: Micro-interaction among computer coordinators and classroom teachers in elementary schools. *Journal of Research on Computing in Education, 28*(1), 29–45.

Franklin, T., Turner, S., Kariuki, M., & Duran, M. (2001). Mentoring overcomes barriers to technology integration. *Journal of Computing in Teacher Education, 18*(1), 26–30.

Gordon, D. (1993). *Descriptions of the sixteen types.* Gainesville, FL: Center for Applications of Psychological Type.

King, R. (1991). *Mentoring: A review of related literature.* Unpublished manuscript. Fort Collins, CO: Colorado State University.

Krupp, J. (1983). Mentoring: A means by which teachers become staff developers. *Journal of Staff Development, 8*(1), 12–15.

Leggett, W. & Persichitte, K. A. (1998). Blood, sweat, and tears: 50 years of technology implementation obstacles. *Tech Trends, 43*(3), 33–36.

Moskal, P., Martin, B., & Foshee, N. (1997). Educational technology and distant education in Central Florida: An assessment of capabilities. *The American Journal of Distant Education, 11*(1), 6–22.

Myers, I (1993). *Introduction to type in organizations: Individual interpretative guide.* (6th ed.). Palo Alto, CA: Consulting Psychologists Press.

Rogers, E.M. (2003). *Diffusion of innovations* (5th ed.). New York, NY: Free Press.

Schrum, L. M. (1995). Educators and the Internet: A case study of technology development. *Computers in Education, 24*(3), 221–228.

Townsend, M. (1997). Computer block—does it exist in the comprehensive secondary school? *National Council for Educational Technology, 28*(4), 3–5.

Trotter, A. (1999, September 23). Training matters: The kids and I learned together. *Education Week, XIX*(4), 44–46.

Van Ast, J. (2000). *Community college induction mentoring program mentor-mentee handbook.* Ames, IA: Iowa State University.

Wickman, F. (1996). *Mentoring: The most obvious yet overlooked key to achieving more in life than you ever dreamed possible.* Columbus, OH: McGraw-Hill Trade.

Wild, M. (1996). Technology refusal: Rationalizing the failure of student and beginning teachers to use computers. *British Journal of Educational Technology, 27*(2), 134–143.

Zachary, L. (2000). *The mentor's guide: Facilitating effective learning relationships.* San Francisco: Jossy-Bass

Zimmerman, I. (2001). Building public support: The politics of technology transformation. In J. LeBaron and C. Collier (Eds.), *Technology in its place: Successful technology infusion in schools* (pp. 99–111). San Francisco: Jossey-Bass.

CHAPTER 11

LESSONS LEARNED

Ann Thompson

As mentoring programs in technology become more common in universities and K–12 environments, it is important that we learn from the work of others. In this book, we have described the implementation of one of the oldest technology mentoring programs in the nation. (Each of the stories told in the book highlights significant aspects of our mentoring program as it has played out in individual cases.) Taken together, the stories suggest themes and lessons for building such programs. As indicated in Chapters 2 and 3, many of these lessons are reinforced by both change theory and the emerging literature on mentoring programs. In this chapter, using elements of Rogers' (2003) diffusion theory described by Sahin in Chapter 2, and major themes from the literature summarized in Chapter 3, we will highlight and generalize the main findings from our work and provide suggestions for the future.

FORMING A COMMUNITY THAT SUPPORTS TRIALABILITY AND OBSERVABILITY OF TECHNOLOGY IS IMPORTANT

The most significant theme we find in our work, and in the literature, is the need to form a community around the mentoring program (see Figure 11.1). Merely assigning students to work one-on-one with faculty will probably not result in a successful program. Mentors need support from each other, and mentees need to be a part of a community of learners. According

Faculty Mentoring: The Power of Students in Developing Technology Expertise, pages 135–146

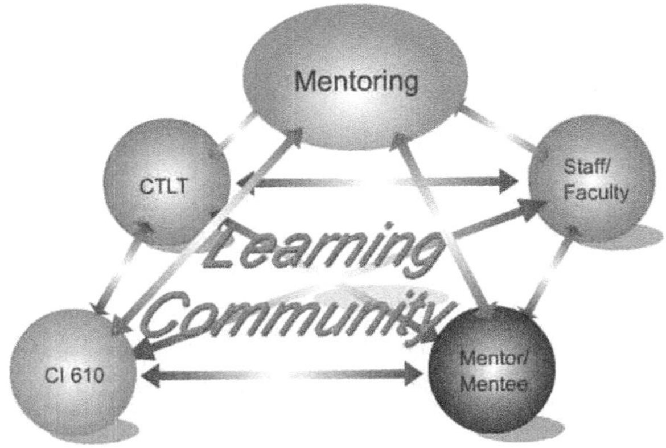

Figure 11.1. The learning community around the mentoring program.

to Stephen and Evans (2000), a nurturing and supportive learning community allows members to exchange ideas, share experiences, and accommodate individual learning styles. In our program, we use mentor/mentee large-group meetings/celebrations and the structure of a formal course to help with this community building. Others have affirmed the need for establishing community in mentoring programs and have suggested specific approaches for establishing community (MacArthur et al., 1995; Sprague, Kopfman & Dorsey, 1998; Thompson, Hansen & Reinhart,1996).

The existence of our Center for Technology in Learning and Teaching (http://www.ctlt.iastate.edu/) (see Figure 11.2) helped provide a home for the community of faculty and graduate students in the program. The mentors worked to help faculty know that their work was part of the mission of the CTLT and that the faculty were part of the CTLT community. This community provides the faculty with the opportunity to try new instructional technologies and to get the simultaneous support when needed (trialability attribute). The importance of the community as a significant base for the successful adoption of these technologies in teacher education programs is a theme that permeates all our work.

Each semester the mentoring program is offered, we begin with a group meeting of mentors and mentees. This initial meeting occurs in the second or third week of the mentoring relationship. Prior to the meeting, the mentoring pairs have had at least one meeting. The initial mentoring meeting is a combination of information sharing and a celebratory event. Each pair introduces itself, with the mentors introducing the mentees and the mentees introducing the mentors. Each pair also describes the goals and projects they have defined for the upcoming semester. As mentioned by Sahin in Chapter 2, goal setting is an important characteristic of Social Learning Theory and is a positive factor in creating collaboration in a com-

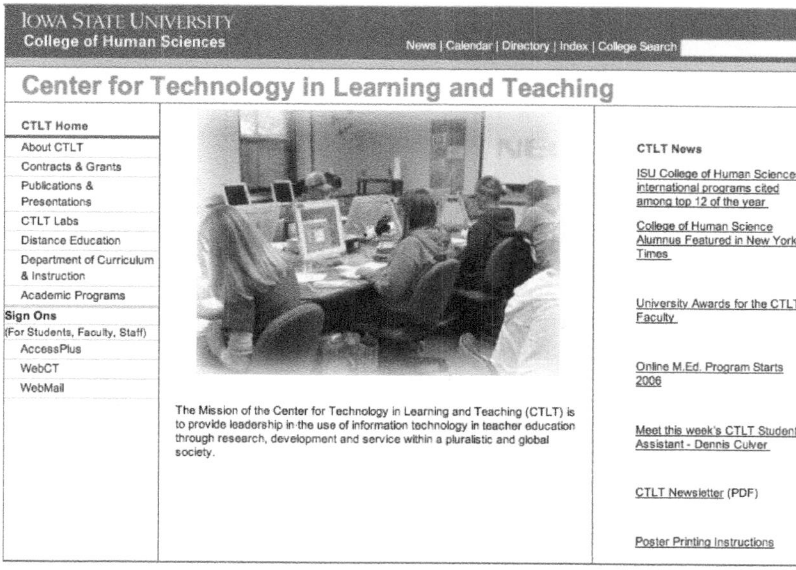

Figure 11.2. CTLT web site.

munity. As seen in Chapters 8, 9, and 10, mutual goal setting helps create a collaborative learning environment in the faculty mentoring program.

In fact, this initial large-group meeting is designed to help form the community of mentors and mentees. At the meeting, all project participants have the opportunity to meet each other and hear about the planned work with technology. Typically, several of the mentoring pairs will get new ideas for their work together from the planned work of others. These meetings also provide the opportunity for faculty who have had mentors in previous semesters to tell the story of their mentoring experiences. These stories are generally very positive and provide added motivation for mentors and mentees new to the program.

Similarly, a final celebration of the events of the semester is held at the end of the semester. Here each mentoring pair reports on the projects they have worked on and, typically, some finished projects are presented. At a recent final celebration, one pair showed a faculty web page that had been developed and another pair showed initial work on a virtual reality environment designed to help students "see" classrooms where they will have field experiences prior to the field experiences (see Figure 11.3). A third group showed digital video of classroom scenes that would be used in methods classes. This final meeting is always a celebration of accomplishment. A common theme in the final meeting is that the mentor-mentee pairs would like to continue their work together as they still have unfinished projects. The CTLT provides both facilities and structures to ensure the continuance of these relationships.

Figure 11.3. Working on creating a virtual classroom.

We see these two sets of meetings as crucial parts of our mentoring programs. Through these meetings, faculty members are able to see the work of others and collect ideas for their own work (observability attribute). They are also able to voice both concerns and successes in their quest to use technology to improve student learning in their classes. Over the years, these meetings have helped in the formation of a community of technology-using faculty who readily share ideas and approaches with one another. Faculty who have had mentors in the past, but who do not have a mentor during a particular semester, are invited to the meetings and frequently attend. These meetings include both interpersonal communication channels and observational learning: two features that are necessary for the successful integration of instructional technology into teaching.

In addition to these "bookend" meetings, the mentors meet each week in a graduate class. In this class, mentors describe their experiences from the prior week and ask for help in problematic situations (see Figure 11.4). Sometimes the challenges discussed are technical, sometimes they are pedagogical, and sometimes they are interpersonal. In all cases, students in the class have the opportunity to learn from the experiences of other students. At the end of a semester, the mentor students have experienced a rich variety of challenges involved with faculty development. They have also had the opportunity to learn how others approach and solve these challenges. In some cases, a class member may attend a mentoring session with a fellow mentor to help solve a particular challenge. These weekly meetings are a

Figure 11.4. CI 610 Technology in teacher education weekly meeting.

significant part of the program which provide mentors with opportunities for support and also help mentors develop a deep understanding of the varied and complex challenges involved in faculty development.

THE MATCH IS IMPORTANT FOR THE ADOPTION OF INSTRUCTIONAL TECHNOLOGY

As the instructor for the graduate course that accompanies our mentoring program, I am also the matchmaker for mentors and mentees. Each semester, I give faculty the opportunity to sign up for a mentor and ask the faculty to give an indication of areas in which they would like to work. I then take this list and work to find matches with the students enrolled in the class. As suggested in the cases in this book, several factors are involved in this match making activity.

My first consideration is the level of the technology use of the faculty member. For a high-end faculty user, I must have a mentor with strong technology expertise. Typically, I have two or three students in the class who have exceptional technology knowledge, and I use these students to work with our more experienced faculty users. Thus, if a faculty member wants to create virtual reality environments for his/her students, I will find a mentor who has the background to work in this area. Faculty members who want to work with WebCT are matched with mentors who have experience in this area.

After I have matched the high-end faculty technology users (usually we only have one or two of these each semester), I then consider subject matter specialization. For example, I attempt to match reading faculty with mentors who have interest and or expertise in this area.

Personality and individual characteristics are also influential in my matching decisions. For example, if I have a faculty member who might be extra demanding of a mentor, I try to find a mentor with exceptionally strong interpersonal skills. I try to match our international graduate students with faculty who show a special interest in working with international students.

To summarize, the matching process is a bit of a hierarchy of decisions, operating with the following considerations:

- subject area interest of the faculty and the mentor (relative advantage attribute)
- potential compatibility of the faculty and mentor (compatibility attribute)
- technology experience level of the faculty and the mentor (simplicity attribute)

Each of these elements of the matching process relates to one of the attributes of innovations. The compatibility of the faculty member and mentor in terms of faculty needs, subject area, and characteristics helps mentors to make the process smooth and show the faculty member that instructional technologies are easy and simple to use. The compatibility of the faculty member and mentor also make it easier for the pair to work on technology applications that have immediate advantage for the faculty member's teaching. Each semester, there is usually at least one match that doesn't work out. The most common reason for the failure of a match is that the faculty member cannot find time to work with the student. When this occurs, I try to meet with the faculty member to see if the problem is solvable. If it is not, I find a new mentoring assignment for the student. Similarly, if the student is not able to meet the expectations of the faculty member, I meet with the mentor and mentee together and attempt to find a solution. If we are unable to find a solution, I will find a new mentee for the student and, if possible, a new mentor for the faculty member.

Since all the mentors are in a class together, they have the opportunity to discuss the challenges in each of their mentoring experiences. Often, other students are able to suggest new approaches and new ideas to students who are having problems. Each of the students in the class learns from the challenges of other students in the class. Occasionally, one of the students in the class will work with another student who is having problems with his/her mentee, and thus we will have a two-on-one model for a short period of time.

The opportunity to share the challenges in the mentoring experiences is a significant factor in working to make the matches successful.

THE PROCESS OF DIFFUSION IS STEADY AND SLOW

Over 14 years, the mentoring program has contributed to the creation of a community of technology using faculty and graduate students. The story of mentoring programs brings to mind the best selling book, *The Tipping Point,* by Malcolm Gladwell. In *The Tipping Point,* the author suggests that many major changes in our society occur relatively quickly once a significant group of people has accepted the innovation. His examples include the wide acceptance of Hush Puppy shoes and the Sesame Street TV program (Gladwell, 2000). Similarly, a mentoring program can involve influential faculty who play critical roles through interpersonal communication channels in reducing faculty uncertainty about instructional technologies and their consequences and, over time, change the culture. We have definitely observed this phenomenon in the growth of our mentoring program over the years. During the first years of the program, only a small percentage of the faculty members in the department participated in the program. With each passing year, however, this percentage grew as those who had participated influenced other faculty in the department.

This culture change will probably not occur in the first or second year of the program, but as more faculty have the opportunity to discover the applications of technology for their teaching (knowledge), a culture of technology-using faculty grows (persuasion) and creates added motivation for others to join in (decision). After 14 years, 29 of the 31 tenure track faculty in our teacher education department have participated in the mentoring program (implementation) and/or taken significant steps in integrating technology into their work (confirmation). Recently, mentor students reported a rather compelling example of this faculty culture when several mentors scheduled a meeting of all the faculty mentees who had indicated an interest in working with WebCT. The original purpose of the meeting was to determine what type of uses the faculty members wanted to make of WebCT in order to assign the appropriate mentor to each faculty member. The mentors reported, however, that the meeting turned into an exciting sharing of faculty work in this area and an opportunity for faculty to learn from the work of other faculty. The mentors reported that they were quite humbled by the faculty expertise and work in this area. I happened upon a second powerful example of a changing department culture last spring. A department secretary told me that we needed to find funds to equip one of our older classrooms with a computer and projector because "none of the faculty want to teach in there." She said that the faculty now demanded technology access for their teaching. I regarded this information as a major triumph.

It is clear that the benefits of mentoring grow over time and that in order to be effective, these programs need to be continued over several years and institutionalized. We use the graduate course as a permanent structure that ensures the continuance of our program. Others have institutionalized changes by requiring faculty to re-design teacher education courses with modifications using technology (Rivers, Eichelberger, & Ho, 2005).

As our stories suggest, faculty progress is generally steady, but slow. Faculty in our program all had many demands on their time and preferred to work on one or two projects each semester they had a mentor. In the program described in this book, most of the faculty mentees have had mentors for more than one semester. One faculty member has had a mentor each of the 14 years the program has been in operation, and her expertise now exceeds that of many of our student mentors. Almost all the mentees in the program express a desire to continue the relationship past the one-semester mark, and in many cases, mentor and mentees have continued these relationships informally.

THERE ARE MUTUAL BENEFITS FOR MENTORS AND MENTEES

When we first began the mentoring program, the main concern was to find an affordable and effective faculty development program. Although it was clear that mentoring would be a valuable learning experience for our graduate students, we did not anticipate the depth of the value of this experience. Most mentoring relationships described in the literature emphasize the mutual rewards for mentors and mentees (Beisser, 2000; Gonzales & Thompson, 1998; Resta, 1998; Thompson, Hansen, & Reinhart, 1996). As evidenced in our stories, mentors find the experience valuable and fulfilling. Finally, mentors report that the mentoring experience expands their own knowledge of technology. Student mentors often learn new computer applications suggested by their faculty mentees. We do not require that mentors have previous knowledge of applications requested by faculty. We only ask that mentors be willing to learn the applications with the faculty. Recently, one of our faculty mentees who teaches a qualitative methods course expressed a desire to learn about a software package for analyzing qualitative data. Although the student mentor had no previous knowledge of the package, she learned to use it with the faculty member. The knowledge and later use of the software program was an unanticipated reward from the mentoring experience. Some have suggested that their mentoring experience was the most powerful learning experience of their graduate career.

One of the rewards frequently mentioned by our mentors is the opportunity to get to know a faculty member and how he/she approaches the teaching/learning process. Students often report learning from their mentoring relationship with faculty. Some of this learning is in the area of pedagogy and some is in the area of the faculty member's content expertise. Some of the learning is also related to obtaining an "inside view" of the life of a faculty member. Since many of our students will become faculty members themselves, this opportunity is highly valued.

A second reward found by mentors in the program is the opportunity to be a contributing part of the technology mentoring learning community. In Chapter 5, Chuang comments on the value of the program for her as an international student. In her story, she describes how her mentoring experience caused her to become an integral part of our community of learners. The mentoring program made it clear to Chuang that she brought valuable knowledge and skill to our program and that she could share this knowledge and skill in a very useful way. Many of our mentors report that the program helps them to understand how much their technology expertise is valued (see Figure 11.5).

Our mentors also suggest that the mentoring experience helps them to envision innovative and appropriate uses of technology in the teacher education program. Most of the mentors come to the program with a relatively sophisticated knowledge of technology, and most of them are relatively new to the curriculum and pedagogy of teacher education. In many cases, the faculty member mentee will suggest new ideas for how a particular technology might help address a specific problem in teacher education. Often, the mentor and mentee pairs are able to work together, share expertise and create innovative uses of the technology that address problems in teacher education. For example, this past semester one of our mentors showed her mentee a virtual reality software package that we had just purchased. Although the mentor could demonstrate the program, she did not have specific ideas about

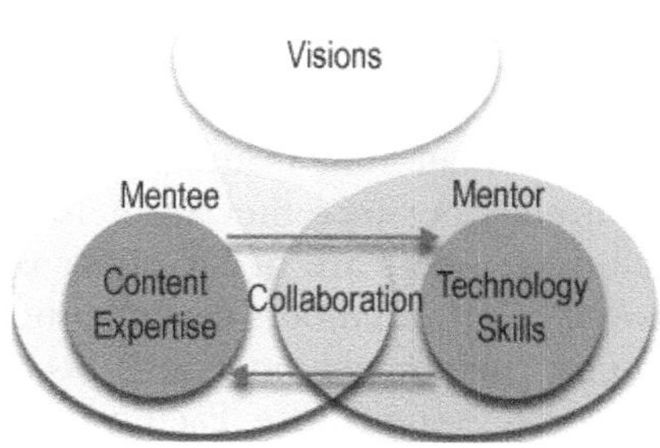

Figure 11.5. Visions created through collaborative efforts between mentors and mentees.

how the software might be used. The mentee, a reading methods teacher, looked at the software and suggested that it could provide a way to preview classroom experiences for her methods students. The mentor and mentee decided to implement this idea and proceeded to take video of classrooms where the methods students would be doing their fieldwork. The video was then transferred into the virtual reality program and the instructor was able to show students many of the details of their classroom arrangements prior to their first visit. With the virtual reality software, the instructor provided a tour of the room for the students and could zoom in on reading centers, bulletin boards, and other areas. Thus, students could discuss and understand issues of classroom arrangement before they began their field experience. Both mentor and mentee were pleased with the virtual reality environment they had created together and with its usefulness in the classroom.

BREAKING DOWN THE HIERARCHY IS NOT DIFFICULT

Zachary (2001) stated that "the traditional hierarchical transfer of knowledge and transformation from an older, more experienced person to a younger, less experienced person, is no longer the prevailing paradigm" (p. 1). All the stories in this book describe the creation of new learning relationships that look somewhat different than the traditional teacher-student relationships. Stories include international students teaching faculty, new graduate students mentoring senior faculty, and classroom teachers mentoring their peers. Each of the relationships described in this book involve learners working in a non-hierarchical relationship to expand both their knowledge of technology and their knowledge of each other.

When I talk with others about the mentoring program described in this book, I am often asked if the faculty members are resistant to receiving help from a graduate student. Breaking down the hierarchy of the teacher-student relationship has never been a problem in the fourteen years of our program and was clearly not a problem in each of the cases in this book. Faculty mentees are enthusiastic about the program and seem to celebrate the knowledge of the graduate students. Faculty members also realize that mentoring is a required part of their graduate student's course work and that it is important to participate fully in the program so that the student can meet his/her requirements. Since they are helping the students complete the course, faculty members are in a familiar position, that of supporting students. Several faculty members have mentioned to me that they feel compelled to attend their weekly meetings because they want their graduate students to do well in the course. Faculty members are able to see the benefits of the program for the students and are pleased to be a part of the students' growth in their ability to help others learn about technology.

RECOMMENDATIONS

Drawing together the major themes we find in our mentoring cases provides some clear suggestions for others implementing student teaching teacher or teacher teaching teacher mentoring programs. Although most of our work has occurred in higher education, the two K–12 cases described in this book suggest that the model is generalizable beyond higher education. Our experience and the literature on faculty mentoring programs indicate that creating a technology mentoring program involves much more than simply assigning students to help teachers learn about technology. These programs go beyond having students' help solve technical problems. They are directed at helping teachers learn to use technology to achieve educational goals.

The following recommendations are based in the cases and literature described in this book and should provide guidance for educators beginning or sustaining faculty or teacher technology mentoring programs:

- establish learning communities of mentors and mentees, providing group opportunities for participants to share both successes and challenges
- pay careful attention to finding compatible matches for mentors (students) and mentees (faculty or teachers)
- ensure that there are rewards for both teachers and students participating in the program
- celebrate and draw attention to the accomplishments of both mentors and mentees
- create structures to ensure that the program is sustainable, recognizing that learning to integrate technology is a multi-year project for faculty or teachers
- provide adequate technology and technology support for participating teachers and students

SUMMARY

All of the lessons learned from our program come together in the creation of new technology learning communities in which students are teaching teachers and all are learning together. In this learning community, the role of the faculty mentoring program is crucial through the stages of the innovation-decision process (knowledge, persuasion, decision, implementation, and confirmation) through showing the attributes of innovations (relative advantage, compatibility, simplicity, trialability, and observability). Ultimately, the learning community formed through the technology mentoring program goes beyond supporting individual faculty member adoption of the innovation to supporting diffusion of the innovation and change throughout the teacher education program. In Epilogue, we emphasize the continuing nature of this process when each of the authors tells her or his story of the ongoing nature of learning communities formed in the mentoring program.

REFERENCES

Beisser, S. (2000). Technology mentorships in higher education: An optimal match for expanding educational computing skills. In B. Gillan & K. McFerrin (Eds.), *Faculty Development.* (ERIC Document Reproduction Service No ED444497).

Gladwell, Malcolm. (2000) The tipping point: How little things can make a big difference (1st ed.). Boston: Little, Brown.

Gonzales, C. & Thompson, V. (1998). Reciprocal mentoring in technology use: Reflecting with a literacy educator. Journal of Information Technology for Teacher Education, 7(2), 163–176.

MacArthur, C. A., Pilato, V., Kercher, M., Peterson, D., Malouf, D., & Jamison, P. (1995). Mentoring: An approach to technology education for teachers. *Journal of Research on Computing in Education, 28*(1), 46–61.

Resta, P. (1998). *Collaborative technologies as a catalyst for changing teacher practices.* Washington, DC: Department of Education. (ERIC Document Reproduction Service No. ED428714).Rogers, E.M. (2003). *Diffusion of innovations* (5th ed.). New York, NY: Free Press.

Rivers, R. A., Eichelberger, A., & Ho, C. (2005). *Turning the tables: Students mentoring faculty to improve university teaching.* Retrieved September 3, 2005 from http://web.jmu.edu/iutconference/Eichelberger&Rivers.PDF

Rogers, E.M. (2003). *Diffusion of innovations* (5th ed.). New York, NY: Free Press.

Sprague, D., Kopfman, K., & Dorsey, S. (1998). Faculty development in the integration of technology in teacher education courses. *Journal of Computing in Teacher Education, 14* (2), 24–28.

Stephen, M. L., & Evans G. D. (2000). Edu-Tech connect: A win-win endeavor. Proceedings of Society for Information Technology & Teacher Education, San *Diego, California, February 8–12, 2000,* 2111–2114.

Thompson, A., Hansen D., & Reinhart, P. (1996). One-on-one technology mentoring for teacher education faculty: Case study reports. In B. Robin, J. D. Price, J. Willis, & D. A. Willis (Eds.), *Technology and Teacher Education Annual, 1996,* (pp. 495–498). Charlottesville, VA: Association for the Advancement of Computing in Education.

Zachary, L. (2001). *Mentoring at a distance: Strategies for success.* U.S. Department of Education Star Schools Project, Distance Learning Resource Network Web Site. Retrieved November 15, 2001, from http://www.dlrn.org/library/dl/mentoring.html.

EPILOGUE

One of the predictable characteristics of the mentor-mentee relationships formed in our program is that these relationships tend not to end when the semester is over. When we have our final meeting to share faculty accomplishments, many faculty members talk about what they plan to do next with technology and ask how they can continue to work with their mentors. Many of our mentors continue to work with their faculty members on collaborative projects, some have published articles with their faculty members on their integration of technology into their courses, and several have worked to establish mentoring programs in other places.

Each of the chapter authors for this book has continued to pursue his/her interest in the mentoring program in different ways and in this chapter, each of these authors provides a view of his/her activities after the formal mentoring course was completed. We have also included a brief professional biography for each author.

FROM THE COORDINATOR OF THE FACULTY TECHNOLOGY MENTORING PROGRAM

Ann Thompson

As a former high school mathematics teacher, I became interested in technology in education through my early experiences with the Logo programming language. The capabilities of Logo to create learner-centered mathematical experiences for children opened my mind to the possibilities that technology could create truly new opportunities for students. Since my early experiences working with Logo, I have continually sought to discover and apply technology experiences that provide new and deeper learning experiences for students. In recent years, the focus of my work has been upon technology

Faculty Mentoring: The Power of Students in Developing Technology Expertise, pages 147–162

applications designed to expand and enhance teacher education experiences. The mentoring program described in this book grew out of my interest in working with teacher education faculty to design meaningful technology applications in teacher education. For fourteen years, I have taught the graduate course that accompanies the mentoring program, placed the mentors with mentees, and enjoyed watching the results of the program.

At Iowa State University, I have worked as a professor in the Department of Curriculum and Instruction, twice as department chair of the Department of Curriculum and Instruction, served as associate dean for research for the College of Education, and founding director of the Center for Technology in Learning and Teaching. Currently, I am a University Professor in the Department of Curriculum and Instruction at Iowa State University.

As I indicated earlier, my involvement in leading the mentoring program has spanned fourteen years. I have worked to change the course each semester and have learned a great deal from both mentors and mentees in the program. This next fall I plan to include more readings on the mentoring process and more information from other technology mentoring programs. I also plan to have more of our graduate student mentors work with content-area professors outside of the Department of Curriculum and Instruction. I have had special requests from the Foreign Language, History, and English departments, and I think that working with subject matter specialists will be a valuable experience for our students.

I believe that the epilogues provide strong testimony for the value of the mentoring program as an ongoing learning experience for all involved. The epilogues demonstrate that the program helps provide new leadership opportunities and new relationships for the graduate students. The mentoring program website (http://www.ci.hs.iastate.edu/mentor/homepage.html) provides further documentation of some of the long-term effects of the program. These effects include publications from both graduate students and faculty, technology applications that are improving the teacher education program, and faculty who continue to use mentors and continue to grow in their technology expertise.

FROM THE MENTORS

Ismail Sahin

After earning my undergraduate degree in mathematics education in Turkey, I was selected by the Turkish Ministry of National Education to pursue my M.S. and Ph.D. degrees with a full scholarship in the United States. After obtaining my M.S. degree in Educational Technology from University of Missouri in Columbia, Missouri, I was admitted to the doctoral program of Curriculum and Instructional Technology at Iowa State University in Ames, IA. Now, I am a faculty member in the Department of Computer and Instructional Technologies at Selcuk University in Turkey. My research areas are faculty development and teacher education.

Being a former technology mentor for a faculty member in the faculty technology mentoring program at Iowa State University, I am the writer of the second chapter of this book. In this chapter, Rogers' (2003) Diffusion of Innovations Theory and its main components, along with the basic elements of Social Learning Theory (Bandura, 1977) and the Concerns-Based Adoption Model (Hall & Hord, 1987), served as a great framework to explain the role of the mentoring program in facilitating the adoption and diffusion of instructional technologies by teacher education faculty members.

I have been inspired by the faculty mentoring program at Iowa State University. I believe faculty use of instructional technologies in teaching is an urgent issue in Turkey and effective faculty development in these technologies will be the response to this issue. Therefore, I would like to apply the mentoring program model at ISU to faculty members back in Turkey.

Since this book mainly presents the cases from the points of view of the graduate students (mentors), I have proposed the idea of creating another book that includes the experiences and perspectives of faculty members (mentees) participating in the faculty technology mentoring program. It will present another perspective on the big picture of this approach to faculty development. This second book will provide further insights into the complex adoption/diffusion process for faculty in the program. In fact, Dr. Thompson and I plan to work on a qualitative research study on the mentee perspectives of the technology mentoring program. In Chapter 2, I mentioned how the mentoring program corresponds with the basic elements of Rogers' (2003) Diffusion of Innovations Theory. In the qualitative research study, we will analyze the role of the technology mentoring program in the adoption and diffusion of instructional technologies of faculty members in the teacher education programs based on the specific elements of this theory.

My major research thrust is now in the area of faculty development and this interest was developed through my initial experiences with faculty technology mentoring. I am currently studying the factors that predict the level of faculty technology implementation and this work is in my dissertation, "Instructional computer use by COE faculty in Turkey: Application of Diffusions of Innovations Theory", and one published article, "Analysis of Predictive Factors that Influence Faculty Members' Technology Adoption Level". I intend to continue this line of research.

Denise Lindstrom

As a sixth grade teacher in Oakland, California, I did not use technology with my students. I became intrigued with the concept on one Back To School Night in the fall of 1997. It was usually expected that few students and parents would actually attend Back to School Night. However, on this night, I stood in the doorway of my empty classroom and watched parents and students, including some of my own parents and students, spill in and out of the classroom next door. The teacher in this classroom had taught her students how to make a multimedia presentation with a program called Kid Pix. Her students were proudly showing them to their parents and everyone else in the classroom. I knew then that I wanted my own classroom to foster that level of enthusiasm. Unfortunately, I had no experience with computers beyond word-processing and some Internet searching. I didn't even use e-mail yet.

In the fall of 1999, I left Oakland and moved to Ames, Iowa to be with my husband who was attending graduate school at Iowa State University (ISU). I took this opportunity to pursue my goal of becoming a more proficient technology user and enrolled in the Curriculum and Instructional Technology Master's Degree program at ISU. Despite my limited computer skills, my experience as a classroom teacher was valued, and I was offered a teaching assistantship for an undergraduate course that taught preservice teachers how to integrate technology into their future classrooms. I also began to work in the Center for Technology in Learning and Teaching (CTLT). The combination of these experiences resulted in a dramatic increase in my skills as a technology user and as a consequence, improved my confidence in my capabilities as an educator.

Dr. Abelson and I still continue our mentor/mentee relationship even though he has been paired with a new mentor for the Fall 2005 semester. He followed up on his interest in using the on-line classroom Blackboard.com. He is using the e-mail feature to communicate with his students, and to post his course procedures, expectations and class schedule electronically instead of using handouts. I helped him learn how to use these features and continue to support him when he runs into trouble using Blackboard.com. He is comfortable in letting me know when he needs help and I look forward to seeing him and being involved with his continued progress in using new technologies in his teaching.

My interest in technology integration continues through my work as a knowledge scout for the Knowledge Innovation for Technology in Education (KITE) PT3 grant. As a knowledge scout, I seek out K–12 technology using teachers and collect their stories of successful technology-based activities. These stories are housed in an on-line database (http://kite.missouri.edu) so that other teachers can read them and learn from each other's experiences. More importantly, the collection of these stories has facilitated my research interest over the past three years. Dr. Neiderhauser, Johannas Strobel, and I use the stories as a data source to understand how the technology-based activities described by these teachers meets the National Technology Standards for Students. We presented our findings at AERA 2005 in a paper titled "Narratives from the front line: Changes in teachers use of technology" and submitted a manuscript titled "Teaching with technology: Standards and reform" in a leading journal in the field of curriculum and instructional technology.

Hsueh-Hua Chuang

I came to Iowa State University as a doctoral student and as a teaching assistant for an undergraduate course, "Introduction to Instructional Technology," in the year 2000 with an M. S. degree in Curriculum and Instructional Technology and five years of high school English as a Foreign Language (EFL) teaching experience in Taiwan. My teaching experience in Taiwan offered me a chance to explore the possibilities of applying technology in foreign language teaching and learning. Studying at ISU provided insights of the role technology can play to reform the teacher education program.

My scholarship focus is on technology and teacher education with an interest in faculty development, especially in one-on-one technology mentoring. I have been involved in the faculty technology mentoring program in the Department of Curriculum and Instruction and have worked with the faculty through the Tech Scholars Program. Tech Scholars is a program connected with Iowa State University's Preparing Tomorrow's Teachers to Use Technology (PT3) grant, which was funded by the U.S. Department of Education. Specifically, this PT3 project provides teacher educators with the necessary support to study and work one-on-one with a technology mentor to develop materials and ideas for integrating technology into teacher preparation courses. I am especially interested in investigating and understanding issues of and barriers to the faculty's continued use and integration of technology in their teacher preparation courses and identifying characteristics and strategies for effective faculty development programs.

Based on the experience in the mentoring relationship with Professor Fuhler, I found it extremely enjoyable to continue working on course development and related tasks with Professor Fuhler through the Tech Scholars program. The Tech Scholars program, affiliated with the Preparing Tomorrow's Teachers to Use Technology (PT3) grant project provides teacher educators with the necessary support to study and work one-on-one with a technology mentor to begin developing materials and ideas for integrating technology into their teacher preparation courses. Professsor Fuhler and I appreciated and trusted each other's ideas about effective strategies for integrating technology to achieve the goal of meaningful teaching and learning. During the collaborative brainstorming process, we explored the possibilities of extending a course on-line, evaluated software packages, and decided what technology would benefit the reading method course.

Professor Fuhler now runs an on-line course with partial assistance from me, uses PowerPoint to assist her lectures, and most of all, manages change well. As her mentor, I gained insightful expertise from a veteran faculty member, which in turn prepares me to envision my own future as a technology educator.

After my initial mentoring experience, I decided that faculty mentoring would become my research emphasis. As a first step in this process, I developed and maintained a web site about the faculty technology mentoring program (http://www.ci.hs.iastate.edu/mentor/homepage.html). The web site documents and archives useful research resources related to the one-on-one faculty technology mentoring approach in faculty development. I presented this web site as part of an invited panel in the Society for Information Technology and Teacher Education (SITE) 2002 conference in Nashville, Tennessee. Drawing on the interest in the technology mentoring program, I started to review the literature and websites to learn more about the mentoring programs as a faculty development approach in higher education and K–12 environments. My first published article, "Faculty Technology Mentoring Programs: Major Trends in the Literature" (Chuang, Thompson, & Schmidt, 2003), in the *Journal of Computing in Teacher Education* is the highlight of my research work with the mentoring program. Later, I continued to collaborate with another faculty mentee from the area of foreign language education on conducting an action research on the use of digital technology in an elementary school foreign language methods course. Recently, we submitted an article, "Use of digital video technology in an elementary school foreign language methods course," to the *British Journal of Educational Technology*, and it has been accepted.

Qian Li

After teaching English as a Second Language for about three years in the University of Science and Technology in Beijing, China, I began to combine different media into my instruction to introduce American culture and history. I was inspired by how the technology enhanced my students' interest in the English language.

Triggered by my interest in educational technology, I came to the U.S.A and enrolled in the Master's program of Instructional Technology at Iowa State University. I developed a good command of computer knowledge and skills. I worked as a graduate assistant for the Department of Curriculum and Instruction. I was a teaching assistant for an undergraduate course entitled "Introduction to Instructional Technology". I taught computer skills and advised preservice teachers as they developed technology projects. I worked as a technology mentor for the faculty members in the department.

Moreover, I became aware of the issues and challenges of computers in schools. This awareness has increased my conviction that technology can enhance and improve teaching and learning if it is used appropriately. My scholarship focuses on assisting faculty designing interactive on-line learning environments. This includes effective on-line instructional design, on-line teaching pedagogy, mentoring, appropriate use of technology in instruction, and dealing with the unique challenges of teaching on-line.

After the semester, our mentoring relationship continued. Dr. Rosenbusch would e-mail me about progress she made by working with WebCT on her own. Frequently, she would ask me for help. With the WebCT site we built, she is now more focused on implementing her activity ideas, such as creating a list serve on WebCT and producing a short video for students to view. She asked me if those activity ideas were doable and easily implemented within WebCT. She gradually gained more management skills using student records on WebCT. I e-mailed her often and also set up extra time for half-hour or hour sessions to provide technical assistance.

For me, it is always a pleasure to know she is using technology to teach more and more deeply. I am excited about every small step she makes in using technology in her teaching. We both learned from our discussions of technical issues and instructional design and provided each other with moral support. This mentoring experience generated another benefit for me during my job interviews for an instructional designer position with universities. One employer valued my experience of mentoring faculty, and I got the job!

Sonmez Pamuk

After earning a B.S. degree in computer education and teaching at a private computer learning center for about three years, I was awarded a scholarship by the Turkish Ministry of National Education to pursue my Master's and Ph.D. degrees in the U.S.A. in the area of instructional technology. To do so, I came to Iowa State University in 2001 as a Master's student in the Curriculum and Instructional Technology program and received my

M.S. degree in 2003. During those years at ISU, I found a great chance to develop and improve my knowledge in several topics related to research and the use of technology in education through courses, presenting at conferences and other professional activities in the department.

My scholarship focus is now mainly on technology and teacher education, professional development of teachers, and educational change models. Currently, as a doctoral candidate, I'm working on my dissertation proposal on whether or not faculty technology mentoring is beneficial to participating technology mentors and identifying strengths and weaknesses of the mentoring structure from mentor perspectives.

The knowledge and experiences I gained during my participation in the Technology and Teacher Education course turned out to be a pivotal stage in my career. It ultimately initiated my interest in faculty technology mentoring and became the subject of my dissertation. For my dissertation I focused on how technology mentoring is as beneficial to the graduates serving as mentors, as it is to the faculty members who are serving as the mentees. To this end, I developed the first technology survey for mentors in the literature.

Currently, I'm working to modify my survey based on the feedback I received from my pilot study and committee members. More importantly, I anticipate being able to make a valuable contribution to the field of teacher education by exploring alternative approaches in mentoring dynamics as virtual life and schooling allow mentors and mentees to operate at a distance.

Comfort Kouadio

I have substantial experience in teaching and working with children and their families and with elementary, secondary, and tertiary school systems. I began my teaching career in Cameroon, West Africa in 1981. Shortly after graduating from the Government Teacher Training College, I worked for the Ministry of National Education in various capacities. I also taught fourth grade for three years, English as a Second Language for two years, and French for one year in a government bilingual secondary school (French/English).

Following these teaching experiences, I decided to broaden my horizons in America because of its advanced system of education and available opportunities. This journey took me to Waldorf College in Forest City, Iowa: then to Minnesota State University at Mankato, where I majored in Psychology with minors in Early Childhood and Parenting Education and obtained a teaching certificate and Parent Educator License; and finally to Iowa State University (ISU) where I pursued a Master's degree in Family and Consumer Sciences specializing in Human Development and Family Studies. I later enrolled in the Curriculum Development and Leadership Program at Drake University, and then returned to Iowa State University. A life-long learner, I am currently pursuing graduate studies at ISU in Curriculum and Instruction with an emphasis on Leadership and Technology. I am also a first grade teacher with the Des Moines Public Schools. At the college level, my teaching experience includes teaching assistantship assignments through the ISU's Curriculum and Instruction Department, and Grand View College's Education Department.

My scholarly and research interests are in the areas of curriculum development, leadership, teacher education and mentoring, technology integration and equity issues. I want to contribute to, and influence change in education through the provision of modern technology-enriched education and professionally prepared and supported teachers.

At the end of the semester, Gwen and I agreed to continue our mentoring relationship until the end of the year. Extending the mentoring relationship allowed us to accomplish her remaining goals. Gwen now has a classroom of her own and continues to use technology tools in lesson planning and incorporates technology into her curriculum. I continue to support and assist her to accommodate her personal technology learning needs as well as those related to curriculum integration.

Currently, I am working on a yearlong technology-mentoring project with the faculty of a small four-year college. The project introduces faculty to underlying theories and frameworks that influence instructional technology as well as pedagogical issues. It also includes training and exposure to relevant computer applications in education, the selection and training of student mentors to work with faculty volunteers, and culminates with an activity involving the documentation and presentation of personal projects. This experience allows me to continue to influence change in education through modern technology.

Jeannette Babcock

Many years ago, I started an undergraduate career at Iowa State College, as it was then known. Unfortunately, illness cut that first higher educational adventure short. In a very roundabout way, I eventually came back to complete a more advanced degree. In the meantime, I completed a Bachelor of Arts degree in English and Education from Drake University and a Master of Science degree in Library Science from the University of Iowa. With college credits from many colleges and universities, I am also a lifelong learner.

My interest in education and technology is nearly as vast as my search for college degrees. I was instrumental in the acquisition and use of the first computers at Johnston High School (Iowa) where I work as a library media specialist. In the years since installing those first three Black Apples, I've served on technology planning committees at local, district, and regional levels. I led computer and technology sessions for 11 years through the Heartland Area Education Agency summer staff development program. I was, and am, a member of educational, library, and technology associations at the local, state, and national levels. I've held offices and served on committees in those organizations at the local and state levels, presented at state level conferences, and attended one national technology conference. I look forward to contributing even more as I complete the Ph.D. program in Curriculum and Instruction at Iowa State University.

The one-on-one technology mentoring program continued to expand at Johnston High School. Each year we made some modifications to the applications, selection process, expectations, and evaluation of this project, which helped to strengthen the program. I also presented a second session at the state technology conference, which in turn provided us with more feedback. Apparently, some public schools are using a similar format for technology staff development, but it is far from common.

Being a part of this group of authors made me realized that I needed to continue to work with Mary on some of the projects that we didn't finish earlier. It is great to have several mentor/mentee teams working in the building, but there are still teachers who have other needs. We will continue to offer alternative forms of staff development and work to make the mentoring program as valuable as possible for the most people. Hopefully, some of the excitement of the mentors and mentees will encourage others to take advantage of this opportunity in future years.

Natalie A. Johnson

I am a passionate, driven, and sociable person who thrives on challenges. Therefore, it was natural that I accepted the challenge to mentor a faculty member integrating technology into his teaching practices. I hail from the small, warm, tropical island of Jamaica with a population of 2.6 million people.

Why would a Jamaican leave the warm shores of her country to study in a place that gets so cold each year? The transition was made (1) because of the reputation of the institution; (2) to face the challenges of graduate school; and (3) for the love of learning. Before coming to graduate school in 1998, I taught high school for six wonderful years. Upon coming to Iowa State University, I pursued a Master's degree in Textiles and Clothing and was a teaching assistant for three semesters.

With my ability to thrive on challenges I decided to pursue doctoral studies in Educational Leadership and Policy Studies with an emphasis in Higher Education. Simultaneously, when the opportunity presented its self for me to do a co-specialization in Curriculum and Instruction Technology I took on the challenge. My educational "quilt" is almost complete and Chapter 10 in this book is one of the pattern pieces in my quilted learning experience.

My scholarly and research interests include several areas; sustainability of technology innovations in institutions of higher education; leadership for stability and change; technology leadership and change; and the area of authentic assessments. My passion for learning will be the driving force behind my success in pursuing my research interests.

The novelty of being a mentor for a faculty member did not wear off at the end of the semester. A quasi-working relationship continued between Dr. Abelson and myself. Each time Dr. Abelson and I met in the hallway, we were able to visit with each other, however briefly. In my opinion, a bond developed between Dr. Abelson and I that would not have developed if I was not engaged in the mentor/mentee relationship. I remember on one occasion, Dr. Abelson asked me to accompany him to the classroom where he was scheduled to teach in the following semester. He wanted to become familiar with the physical layout and structure of this "technology friendly" classroom ahead of time.

Although I was no longer assigned to Dr. Abelson as his mentor (and my final paper was already turned in), I was happy to accompany him to the classroom. Together we looked at the facilities so that Dr. Abelson could become familiar with the set-up. This activity went very well because our goal was accomplished. Conversely, at the beginning of the new semester, there was a change in the classroom assignment, hence, Dr. Abelson did not teach in that room. Satisfactorily, he was rescheduled to teach in a classroom in which he was comfortable and familiar. The mentor/mentee relationship, formed three semesters ago, definitely did not end and there are indicators suggesting it will go on in an informal way for more semesters to come.

FROM THE MENTEES

Carol Fuhler

I have been incredibly fortunate to be the recipient of such fine mentoring over the past two years. I can say with all honesty that I would not have been tempted to tackle so many new technological adventures if it hadn't been for my confidence in my mentor, Hsueh-Hua. She came to our mentoring appointments ready to work on an application I was brave enough to try, having done her homework ahead of time. For example, we worked on Blackboard.com initially, and Hsueh-Hua helped me set my course up. Then, she continued to troubleshoot problems throughout the semester. Just when I was feeling comfortable with the basics, Blackboard.com underwent a revision. After consulting with each other, we decided to move on to WebCT the following semester. Hsueh-Hua again explained the basics of a much more confusing format and designed the course for me once more. No matter what the project was, teaching or creating early Power Point lectures or working together on my first I-movie, she has been there to lead the way, one unintimidated step at a time. I'll have to admit, I was most reassured when we'd hit a rare technological roadblock that even stumped my mentor! I realized then, as I do on nearly a daily basis, that staying one step ahead of technological change is a life-long process.

When I look back over the time I have been involved in the mentoring program, it is pleasing to see that I've made some progress. I never would have attempted to learn the applications I now understand if I had had to do it on my own. I relished the one-on-one teaching, the patience of my mentor when I was frustrated, her constant willingness to drop in for an unscheduled few minutes to get me beyond a dilemma, and her continued support, even though I now have a new mentor. She will always be my primary mentor, in my mind, at least. I have grown comfortable with her as my teacher and always knowing that she would not laugh at my ineptness—smile a little, perhaps, but never discourage me with a laugh. I am positive that many other teachers would be way ahead of their current technological understanding if only they had a mentoring program and a fine mentor to assist them.

Marcia Rosenbusch

It was interesting for me to read Qian Li's reflections on the semester in 2000 when we worked together. That is now five years ago, and I am pleased to see the progress I have made since that time with Qian Li's help again in Fall 2001 and with help from other technology mentors.

I had forgotten the frustrations in learning the new WebCT system (how could I have forgotten that?) and now I use it with relative ease. It took me, however, until the fall semester 2002 to feel like I had defined how to use WebCT with my methods course. I had been putting parts of my syllabus on WebCT since we had first worked together, but since students also had a paper syllabus, that did not seem to make a lot of sense. I had begun having students use WebCT Discussion to report on some course assignments to the whole class and I also had used Chat in a limited, and not too successful, way on two occasions in the fall of 2001. But I remained tentative about what WebCT could mean for my course.

When Qian Li helped me move from my antiquated electronic grading system to Excel with reporting on WebCT, I finally realized the power of WebCT. Students could have access to their grades as soon as I had entered them in to the electronic grade book, or whenever I should decide they should have access. That is a powerful tool! I became much more enthusiastic about WebCT after keeping my grade book in that system. I decided to try the university library web reserve system for course readings and loved it. I also began using more Internet sites as source material for the course. I was thrilled when Qian Li helped me develop a beautiful home page for the WebCT course. I have never liked the graphics that WebCT provides so that made an important difference in how I felt about the course website.

Encouraged by what I had learned, and believing that having both a paper and WebCT syllabus was redundant, in fall semester 2002, I moved to an entirely electronic syllabus. A few days before class began, however, I became nervous about my decision when I read the departmental guidelines specifying that instructors are to provide students with a syllabus the first day of class. I checked with my department chair who encouraged me to provide a least a few pages of the syllabus and the grading system on paper as a handout. I did so but I was amazed that not one student complained of not having received a complete paper syllabus. They are using WebCT without any problems.

I had begun exploring the use of digital video clips of elementary school foreign language classes with my students last year. Students viewed the clips with a partner, analyzed them to answer guiding questions and reported on their analysis to the class. I continue to use the digital video clips this year and have posted some of these clips on my course WebCT site. I will use Chat this semester to connect small groups of students with practicing elementary school foreign language teachers to discuss their analysis of the digital video clips. Now, students access all of the readings electronically, although I still provide paper handouts for some work in class. For the first time this semester the students are having amazingly lively discussions about the course readings on WebCT, with questions posed and the discussion monitored by students. I have found that these discussions provide me with valuable insight into their reactions to and thinking about the readings. I now cannot imagine how I would teach my course without WebCT!

Mary Ohaver Moermond

My mentee/mentor experience with Jeannette gave me the skills to use more technology, the courage to assign my students more technology projects, and motivation to complete the National Board Certification process. One new project that worked especially well was a Web search on modern-day Guinea. The students each received a copy of the 1996 *Culturgram* on the Republic of Guinea. This four-page brochure, published by Brigham Young University, provided information on Guinea's cultural attitudes and priorities, people, customs, everyday life, and social institutions. The students were each assigned a portion of the *Culturgram* to research on the Web to see if this information had changed over the last six years. In this endeavor, the technology of the Internet supported and extended the students' learning. They researched the information on French-language Web sites, and then shared this information with the class through oral reports. The research, in turn, the students' presentations, encouraged insight into this culture and maximized their opportunity to use French in context. Furthermore, their access to technology was an important component of their learning environment. By comparing the written brochure and the information on the Internet, the students learned about contemporary life in Guinea and explored links between language learning and the real world.

Recently, I tried for National Board Certification. As part of the certification process, I had to submit four different teaching portfolios, one of which was entitled, "Documenting Accomplishments: Contributing to Student Learning." The third accomplishment in my collection of eight was the collaborative technology project completed with Jeannette. Throughout the whole certification process, all fifteen of the standards encouraged the use of technology in class. My experiences with the mentor/mentee project helped me with ideas and examples for this portion of the certification portfolio.

Geoff Abelson

Mentor/mentee relationships are not restrained by time. In fact, the nature of the bond between mentor and mentee may remain over many years when it is mutually reinforcing. My relationship with my mentor, Denise, has continued for more than three years. I attribute this to mutual trust, my need to expand the use of technology, and Denise's generosity to share, support and teach. Initially, my goal was to learn to prepare and implement PowerPoint presentations. During Denise's first semester as a graduate student and mentor, I developed enough competency to do "solo" PowerPoint presentations. Denise, subsequently, was available for "as needed" consultations throughout the academic year. The next fall, I asked Denise to help me learn a technology based support system for course and student management. Each semester, I teach a class of 300 students, and I wanted to learn more technology to facilitate the course for the students and myself. At the time, the university had subscribed to WebCT and was promoting it for faculty adoption. Denise convinced me that Blackboard.com had the attributes I needed in a support system, and that WebCT was cumbersome to implement. I agreed to learn Blackboard.com to avoid what I viewed as unnecessary obstacles. Denise assisted me in establishing and implementing Blackboard.com. Denise continued to be accessible and help me solve transient problems with both PowerPoint and WebCT.

This fall, I abandoned the use of Blackboard.com because of newly imposed subscription charges. Blackboard.com had been free. Currently, I am in the throes of learning to implement WebCT. Although, other graduate students have been assigned to assist me with WebCT, I am comfortable to continue to depend on Denise to complement and supplement the efforts of others. And Denise has been unselfish in continuing the mentoring process.

CONCLUSION

As the Epilogue suggests, our faculty mentoring program goes far beyond a one semester experience for faculty and graduate students. Both value the experience and the learning community that has formed around the experience. Ultimately, the major product of the program is the meaningful integration of technology into the teacher education program, and we are working to collect evidence of this integration and its effectiveness from our students. Our research agenda now includes following our teacher education students into their first years of teaching to study the effects of the faculty integration of technology into the preservice program. Jon Clausen, in his dissertation entitled, "Technology integration and new teachers' instructional practice: Case studies of two beginning teachers' technology use", provides a qualitative description of two first year teacher's experiences with technology. Both of the first year teachers in Clausen's study were graduates of our teacher education program and both made extensive use of technology during their first year of teaching. Clausen described the influence of the teacher education program on one of the students:

> When asked about whether her teacher education program influenced her current instructional practices, Kim stated, "Oh, almost all of it" (end of year interview). Kim frequently commented about how she used the resources and methods modeled by her teacher education program instructors. These images of teaching and how to use technology transferred into her first year of teaching. (Clausen, 2005, p. 113)

We will continue to implement and study our faculty mentoring program and work to share our evolving experiences and approaches with others. We will share both our developing practice and research through publications and on our web site, and urge readers to stay tuned in to this unfolding story.

REFERENCES

Bandura, A. (1977). *Social learning theory.* Englewood Cliffs, NJ: Prentice Hall.

Chuang, H., Thompson, A., & Schmidt, D. (2003). Faculty technology mentoring program: Major trends in the literature. *Journal of Computing in Teacher Education, 19*(4), 101–106.

Clausen, J. (2005). Technology integration and new teachers' instructional practice: Case studies of two beginning teachers' technology use (Doctoral dissertation, Iowa State University, 2005).

Hall, G.E., & Hord, S.M. (1987). *Change in schools: Facilitating the process.* New York, NY: State University of New York Press.

Rogers, E.M. (2003). *Diffusion of innovations* (5th ed.). New York, NY: Free Press.

9 781593 115708

Printed and bound by CPI Group (UK) Ltd, Croydon, CR0 4YY

15/09/2026

14962367-0006